TRACING AN(
BEDFORD....

Colin R Chapman

SECOND EDITION

Colin Chapman, born in neighbouring Northampton, lived in Bedford for the first twenty years of his life and was educated at Bedford School for eleven years. He has been interested in local, social and family history since the age of seven after discovering a Family Bible in his grandparents' attic. He is a son of Don and Edna Chapman, some of whose ancestors originate in Bedfordshire, others coming from adjacent Huntingdonshire, Buckinghamshire and Northamptonshire. Besides being an industrial chemist and nuclear engineer by profession, Colin Chapman has lectured world-wide on British social and family history since 1980; he was the first Western genealogist to be invited to speak in the former Czechoslovakia following the warming of East-West relations in 1989. He has spoken in Berlin, Heidelberg, Geneva, Paris, Vienna, Jakarta and throughout Britain and the Channel Isles on genealogically-related topics and regularly undertakes lecture tours across Canada, the United States of America, Australia and New Zealand using examples from Bedfordshire archives to illustrate his talks. He originated the three-letter Chapman County Code for British Isles counties which formed the basis for a British Standard and now an International Standard, ISO-3166. He is the author of *Tracing Your British Ancestors, Tracing Ancestors in Northamptonshire, Tracing Ancestors in Rutland, Marriage Laws, Rites, Records & Customs, The Growth of British Education & Its Records, Ecclesiastical Courts Officials & Records, Pre-1841 Censuses & Population Listings in the British Isles, How Heavy How Much & How Long?* (weights, money and other measures) and *Using Newspapers & Periodicals* (in historical research). He is President of the Gloucestershire Family History Society, President of the Bristol & Avon Family History Society and an honorary member of the Bedfordshire Family History Society. He is a life Vice-President of the international Federation of Family History Societies, a Fellow of the Society of Genealogists and a former member of its executive committee.

Published by
LOCHIN PUBLISHING
6 Holywell Road, Dursley, GL11 5RS, England

First Edition 1995
Second Edition 1998
Copyright of the Lochin Publishing Society 1995, 1998

British Library Cataloguing in Publication Data
A catalogue record for this book is available from the British Library.
ISBN 1 873686 12 9

Contents

Using This Book Successfully

If you have ancestors who lived in Bedfordshire, or if you want to use sources in Bedfordshire today to trace ancestors whose origins were elsewhere, this book will be especially useful to you. The content also offers vital assistance to local and social historians using records of past generations to recall and reconstruct communities and conditions from previous eras.

The Prelude offers guidance for beginners to genealogy and family history; even the "old hands" may care to skim through this for revision and for some up-to-date facts. The Postscript reminds you to write-up the results of your research for the benefit of others and it points you to further guidance. The remaining Chapter Headings and Contents Page, used in conjunction with the Index, will enable every reader, beginners and more advanced researchers alike, to locate items to interest them in this book.

Throughout the text, bibliographic references and suggestions for further reading are identified by [1], [2] etc. and expanded upon on page 57. To help your research, references to documents and classes of archives held at the Bedford County Record Office (CRO) are indicated within {}, such as {BP 43/1-13} and {ED}. Where <name> or <place> etc. are shown as part of a reference, you must replace these with the specific name of the family, person, place or object in which you are interested to procure the item for your use at the CRO.

The list of civil and ecclesiastical parishes in Chapter 5 is interleaved with hamlets for those of you, local and family historians, who have found only such names during your research. In every case, by using the references provided, you will be able to locate the appropriate archives in the County Record Office.

A map of Bedfordshire and its parishes in 1880 is on page 52.

Acknowledgement

The request for this book came from Chris Pickford, Bedfordshire's County Archivist, who had seen a similar publication of mine for an adjacent county. Mr Pickford combed through the draft text and offered many suggestions and provided references that I had overlooked. Without his encouragement and vigilance this book would have been the poorer in both detail and the breadth of records identified within the archives in his care.

Prelude: Hints for Beginners to Family History

Start with your immediate family. Quiz your older relatives on any family stories and ask for any documentation; certificates, newspaper cuttings, photograph albums, diaries and notebooks tucked away in cupboards and drawers may give you useful clues. Write down or record on video or audio tape the memories of your family and others in the localities frequented by your ancestors. Now work backwards from yourself....

> ➢ *See also Tracing Your British Ancestors. Colin R Chapman. Lochin Publishing. 1996.*

You have a birth certificate from the civil registration system (see page 15) showing at least the name of your mother and probably your father's name also. Assume you are the oldest child and your parents married around the time of your birth, estimate their wedding date; now obtain a marriage certificate from the same system and see the exact date of the marriage, your parents' ages and addresses, and the names and occupations of their fathers. With information on their ages you can obtain their birth certificates. You can repeat this process back to the beginning of civil registration in England and Wales on 1 July 1837, providing you with several surnames of people from whom you are directly descended.

> ➢ *Original indexes at Family Records Centre, 1 Myddelton Street, London EC1R 1UW.*

> ➢ *Microform indexes of births, marriages and deaths (1837-1983) available at Bedford Central Library and of births (1862-1906), marriages (1860-1903) and deaths (1864-1903) at the Family History Centre at Luton; more complete sets are held at the Family History Centre in Northampton and the CRO in Cambridge (see Chapter 7).*

> ➢ *Copies of certificates available by post: OPCS, General Register Office, Postal Applications Section, PO Box 2, Southport, Merseyside, PR8 2JD.*

Now look through the National Genealogical Directory (NGD), the Genealogical Research Directory (GRD), the British Isles Genealogical Register (BigR) - Bedfordshire section and the Directories of Members' Interests for the Bedfordshire Family History Society (BFHS). These publications indicate who else is researching names and places that may coincide with your interests.

> ➢ *NGD: ed. Iris Caley, published annually from 1979 to 1992.*

> ➢ *GRD: eds. Keith A Johnson & Malcolm R Sainty, published annually since 1981.*

> ➢ *Big R: ed. John Perkins. Federation of Family History Societies. 1994, 1997.*

> ➢ *BFHS Directory of Members' Interests: published in 1977, 1983, 1985 & 1993.*

Next use the addresses from the civil registration certificates in conjunction with 19th Century census returns (see page 10) to discover other family members, occupations and birthplaces, possibly in Bedfordshire parishes, and even back in the 18th Century. Consult the indexes to the 1881 and 1851 census returns prepared by Family History Societies and some local history societies. Now read the main text of this booklet.

> *Original and microform copies of census returns for 1841, 1851, 1861, 1871, 1881 and 1891 are available at the Public Record Office (PRO), and the Family Records Centre (sometimes known as Myddelton Place), Myddelton Street, London.*

> *Microfilm copies of returns for the entire county for 1841 to 1891 available at the CRO and in the Local Studies Library at Bedford Central Library (BCL).*

> *Microfilm copies of returns for the south of the county for most census years are available at Luton Library; see Chapter 7.*

> *Census indexes are available for reference at the CRO or for purchase from the Bedfordshire Family History Society (BFHS); (see foot of this page).*

Record, in a book or file (paper or computer), what you discover. Use a system that you, and hopefully others, can later retrieve and add to. Decide if you are going to attempt to trace all your ancestors, on both your father's and mother's sides, or to record all references to a particular surname (in which case the Guild of One-Name Studies may be able to help you). You should also decide whether to produce a family history (with details on your ancestors' lives and homes, even their appearances and acquaintances) or compile a family tree or pedigree chart of a fundamental genealogy.

> *Guild of One-Name Studies, The Registrar, Box G, 14 Charterhouse Buildings, Goswell Road, London, EC1M 7BA.*

Consider joining the Bedfordshire Family History Society. This Society, besides publishing quarterly journals with articles on individuals, families and parishes in Bedfordshire, holds monthly meetings in Bedford, and undertakes projects such as indexing census returns and transcribing and indexing memorial inscriptions (see page 23). Go to one of their meetings where the Society members will be pleased to help you; many of them also have ancestors outside of Bedfordshire and so can advise you if you are in that position as well.

> *Contact The Secretary, BFHS, PO Box 214, Bedford, MK42 9RX.*

> *For a complete list of all county Societies, send a SAE to the Administrator, Federation of Family History Societies, The Benson Room, Birmingham & Midland Institute, Margaret Street, Birmingham, B3 3BS.*

Bedfordshire's Civil and Ecclesiastical Areas
A Potted History

Bedfordshire anciently comprised several Hundreds, each consisting of Townships in which a number of families lived. Over the centuries townships with a church and priest evolved into Parishes whilst smaller townships became Hamlets. One or more townships were also grouped within a Manor. The hundreds gradually lost their importance, although in some cases parliamentary constituencies embraced similar areas, and the County (Norman-French for Shire) became a more significant unit. Larger centres of population became known as Towns with smaller numbers of people living in Villages. Most towns were Boroughs, the larger being County Boroughs, having similar powers to a County. The term City, in England, describes a town with a Cathedral of the Established Church, irrespective of its population size.

Bedfordshire parishes and hamlets are identified in Chapter 5. There are no cities in the county. Hundreds are identified in Chapter 6, and the manorial system and Bedfordshire boroughs are mentioned in Chapter 4. The shape of Bedfordshire (see the map on page 52) has remained substantially unaltered since the Middle Ages. Minor local government and parliamentary boundary alterations and transfers of parishes between adjacent counties during the 19th and 20th Centuries are described in the next paragraph. Prior to 1974, following the 1972 Local Government Act, Bedfordshire was the fourth smallest county in England.

For parliamentary administration the Tetworth hamlet of Everton was transferred to Huntingdonshire in 1832, but not fully implemented for civil administration until 1844 when part of Ickleford was also transferred to Hertfordshire and parts of Meppershall and Studham were transferred to Bedfordshire from Hertfordshire. Aspley Heath civil parish was created in 1883 and 1885 from parts of Aspley Guise (Bdf) and Wavendon (Bkm). The 1888 Local Government Act enabled Swineshead to be added from Huntingdonshire and Markyate to be transferred to Hertfordshire; the transfers actually took place in 1896/97 and 1907. Caddington, partly in Bedfordshire and partly in Hertfordshire, was split into two civil parishes in 1894, one in each county. In 1896 Tilbrook was transferred to Huntingdonshire (and Swineshead from Huntingdonshire). Kensworth and part of Whipsnade were transferred from Hertfordshire to

Bedfordshire in 1897 when Holwell was transferred to Hertfordshire. An Alterations of Boundaries Order, taking effect in 1907, transferred parts of the Hertfordshire parishes of Flamstead, Little Gaddesden, Harpenden, Markyate and Offley to Bedfordshire. The parish of Staploe was created from part of Eaton Socon in 1965 when the remainder of Eaton Socon was transferred to Huntingdonshire, Everton's boundaries were re-arranged and Linslade was transferred from Buckinghamshire. In 1974 most Huntingdonshire parishes were transferred to Cambridgeshire when the former county was absorbed into the latter. Small areas were transferred to or from the county under the Bedfordshire, Buckinghamshire and Cambridgeshire (County Boundaries) order, 1991.

The Christian Church in England and Wales was organised for administrative purposes into the Provinces of Canterbury (in the south) and York (in the north), each headed by an archbishop; the Archbishop of Canterbury held the senior post of Primate and was originally the Pope's representative in Britain. Each province was organised into dioceses (or sees) headed by a bishop based in the cathedral city of the diocese. Dioceses were organised into archdeaconries, headed by an archdeacon. The archdeacon looked after several rural deaneries, which consisted of parishes, the townships mentioned above where a church had been built. In each parish the priest or incumbent, a clergyman, who was a vicar, a rector or a perpetual curate, administered the Christian sacraments and conducted services in Latin. Children were baptised into the Christian faith, marriages were solemnized by the clergy and the dead were buried according to ceremonies and prayers prescribed from Rome. Some very small areas throughout the country, including some in Bedfordshire, were exempt from this administrative system.

At the Protestant Reformation, which swept across Europe in the 15th and 16th Centuries, Henry VIII was declared titular head of the Anglican Church and so the Church in England became the established Church of England. The organisational structure of parishes, rural deaneries, archdeaconries, dioceses and provinces was largely retained (including the exempt areas) although six new dioceses were created in 1541. During the reign of Edward VI, however, the forms of services were changed and the Book of Common Prayer in English was introduced. The exempt areas became known as Peculiars (see below). England has remained nominally Protestant since 1547, and gradually more tolerant, apart from a brief return to Catholicism during the reign of Mary

(1553-1558); although during the Commonwealth (1649-1660) the civil authorities took over most of the secular duties of the Church - including the solemnization of matrimony.

Bedfordshire (apart from Everton parish, see Chapter 5) fell entirely within the Archdeaconry of Bedford, itself initially in the Diocese of Lincoln and the Province of Canterbury. In 1837 Bedford Archdeaconry was transferred to Ely Diocese, and in 1914 was transferred to St Albans Diocese, still within the Province of Canterbury. The rural deaneries in Bedfordshire were originally Bedford, Clapham, Dunstable, Eaton, Fleete and Shefford, but in 1866 were reorganised into Ampthill, Bedford, Biggleswade, Dunstable, Felmersham, Fleete, Luton, Riseley and Shefford. Deaneries are not considered further in this book as all their activities were historically within the Archdeacon of Bedford's close control.

The parish was used as a unit of both civil and of ecclesiastical administration, whose needs were not quite the same. There are, therefore, some instances of civil parishes without a church, Brogborough for example, and some ecclesiastical parishes, such as Caldecote, having no civil jurisdiction. Sometimes a civil and an ecclesiastical parish cover an almost identical area but have different names, e.g., Aspley Heath and Woburn Sands. In some cases two ecclesiastical parishes, e.g., Dean parish and Shelton parish, are combined to form one civil parish, Dean and Shelton. During the 19th and 20th Centuries additional civil and ecclesiastical parishes were created to meet the requirements of increasing populations in some areas. Occasionally, however, two ecclesiastical parishes were combined into one larger ecclesiastical parish and one church closed, e.g., Tempsford and Little Barford - the latter being made redundant in 1972; but more commonly the benefices (church livings and incumbencies) were combined while the individual parishes remained separate, e.g., Hulcote and Salford. All Bedfordshire parishes are identified in Chapter 5 and shown on page 52.

There were two Peculiars in Bedfordshire outside the jurisdiction of the Bishop of Lincoln (and Ely): Biggleswade and Leighton Buzzard (which included the hamlets of Billington, Eggington, Heath & Reach and Stanbridge). Woburn also claimed exemption and the Dukes of Bedford exercised some, but not all, accepted ecclesiastical rights. All peculiars were abolished in 1858.

1. Information Already Available

Whatever aspect of history is your main interest, do not neglect the published or recorded work and research of others. Family historians can glean much from local histories while community historians would be foolish to ignore details made available by genealogists. Transcribed, translated and published material and indexes and finding aids should always be consulted before looking at original records. Family and local historians would be wise to refer to directories of pedigrees and location interests to discover if anyone else is researching the same names or parishes, with the intent to share the results of the research. There is little sense in duplicating the work of others or repeating what has already been achieved. Obviously, you will want to check other people's research; and not a few genealogies published towards the end of the 19th Century were based on fantasy rather than fact. However, even most amazing tales contain an element of truth, and published materials, particularly if indexed, are excellent starting points.

The *Victoria County History* for Bedfordshire (*VCH*), in three volumes with an index and available in most large reference libraries, has some excellent background material on the county and its people. Joyce Godber's *History of Bedfordshire* [1] published in 1969, has many references to individuals and families, as do the three volumes of *Bedfordshire Notes & Queries*, published in 1886-93. This county is particularly fortunate in having L R Conisbee's extensive and comprehensively arranged *Bedfordshire Bibliography* (1962-75) [2], which itemises many thousands of publications.

The Bedfordshire Historical Record Society (BHRS) has been publishing annual volumes since 1913 with some quarto volumes in 1914-17. BHRS publications include many important genealogical, as well as social and local history items, and refer to other sources. Relevant volumes are identified in subsequent chapters. The Bedfordshire Family History Society (BFHS), founded in 1977, publishes a quarterly journal and regularly updates the lists of surnames and parishes in which its members are interested. The proceedings and publications of the Bedfordshire Architectural and Archaeological Society (established 1847 and now renamed the Bedfordshire Archaeological Society) have many articles of interest to family and local historians, as does the *Bedfordshire Magazine*, published quarterly since 1947 (an index to the first 20 volumes was published in 1987). Many local history groups in the county, including the Local History Association, publish newsletters and magazines. The addresses of their secretaries may be obtained from the County Record Office. Even the annual publications of the Bedfordshire Natural History Society and Field Club have some items relating to historical research. National publications such as the *Genealogists' Magazine, Family Tree Magazine, Local Historian, Local Population Studies* and *Local History* are available in Bedfordshire.

The major repository in Bedfordshire of local and national, original and secondary material is the County Record Office (CRO) which has published a quarterly *Newsletter* since 1987 with some helpful articles on archival sources. There are valuable collections of historical material in the Local Studies Library at Bedford Central Library (BCL) and in some public libraries throughout the county (see Chapter 7 for addresses of those with important local material). The [Mormon] Family History Centre in Luton, also listed in Chapter 7, has microform copies of some indexes to births, marriages and deaths for England and Wales for the 19th Century (see page 2) and of census returns for the same century; this Centre also has other material useful in genealogical and local history research, not only for Bedfordshire but for many other British and overseas areas. Bedfordshire parishes are well represented in the International Genealogical Index (see page 23), and copies of all the county's parish registers (see Chapter 3) are available in hard copy or microform at the CRO, BCL and at Luton Library and some other libraries in the county. The museums in Bedford and Luton and other locations merit a visit to study their artefacts, although some of their documents are now at the CRO. The addresses of these repositories (some open only by appointment) are given in Chapter 7.

Some Bedfordshire material, especially records created by the Crown or national government, is available only at the Public Record Office (PRO) or among various manuscript collections of the British Library in London. Some classes of these records have been microfilmed and copies are available at the CRO while other items have been transcribed, translated where necessary, and published - and are also available at the CRO. There are instances, even so, when you will need to look at records out of the county to trace individuals, families and ancestors in Bedfordshire.

2. Where Did Your Ancestors Live ?

Poll Books and Electoral Registers

If your ancestors were landowners, not necessarily part of the gentry, they (but only males could vote until 1918) would have been entitled to a vote at a Parliamentary Election. Candidates were voted for openly on polling days (a secret ballot is a modern concept) and those with the greatest number of votes declared the elected Members of Parliament. Bedfordshire originally had two parliamentary divisions or constituencies, Bedford Borough and Bedfordshire. The CRO has Poll books with names, arranged under Hundreds, of those who voted and for whom they voted for the years 1685, 1705, 1715, 1722, 1727, 1734, 1774, 1784, 1807, 1820, 1826, 1831, 1857, 1859, and 1872. The CRO also holds Poll Books of Bedford for the years 1640, 1705, 1721, 1725, 1727, 1730, 1790, 1830, 1835, 1837, 1841, 1847, 1857, and 1868. Bedford Town Hall (see Chapter 7) has Bedford Poll Books for 1832, 1852, 1859 and 1865. Following the 1832 Electoral Reform Bill, the entitlement to vote was extended and Electoral Registers were introduced. The CRO has registers {RE} for 1834-1970s (apart from 1940-45) for all Parliamentary Divisions in Bedfordshire.

Directories and Gazetteers

Towards the end of the 18th Century court and trade directories were published throughout the country, following the successes of London directories. For over 100 years the names of those who paid the publishers appeared more prominently in such directories; names included are predominately of landowners, the gentry, clergy and tradespeople, shopkeepers, carriers and publicans. County directories initially contained the principal towns and listed subscribers, often in alphabetical order. Gazetteers, and some directories, often included historical as well as topographical notes on a county. Some directories and gazetteers were arranged by Hundreds, later publications included smaller towns and villages, though rarely every parish, arranged in alphabetical order; large towns (e.g. Bedford) listed people by street and house numbers. Some directories included even street indexes and as the 20th Century progressed every householder was listed. The CRO has Trade Directories and Gazetteers of Bedfordshire between 1785 and 1940 and from 1866 to 1975 for Bedford Borough with Kempston. All are on the open shelves in the Search Room at the CRO. Luton Public Library has copies of

Luton directories from 1896 to 1975. Initially Pigot, and from the mid-19th Century, Kelly were the principal publishers of Bedfordshire directories.

Census Returns

National censuses have been taken every ten years since 1801, apart from 1941. The enumerations of households were originally conducted by counties and parishes, but from 1841 the Registration Districts set up in 1836 were used. The Registration District in which each Bedfordshire parish is located is identified in Chapter 5. The early returns required only numbers of males and females in five-year age bands to be noted; from 1841 the names, ages to the nearest five years, rounded downwards, and if born in the same county (Y) or not (N), were recorded, household by household. From 1851, again by households, the names, actual age, occupation, birthplace and relationship to the head of the household for every individual were required. Only from 1841 were copies of the returns required in London. Nevertheless, some returns for Bedfordshire districts, listed in Chapman (see [3] and [4]), with names and ages of individuals for 1801, 1811, 1821 and 1831 have survived and are at the CRO.

However, censuses and lists of people were taken nationally and locally long before this. The earliest listing is the Domesday Survey of 1086. Many lists were made to raise revenue and so are taxation or subsidy rolls or lists. Poll Taxes from 1377, Hearth Taxes from 1662, Marriage Duty Taxes from 1694, Window Taxes from 1696, Land Taxes (from 1750 for the south west of Bedfordshire) and Horse Taxes, Dog Taxes, Hair Powder Taxes, to name only a few. Some lists (Militia Lists and Muster Rolls) were to identify who was fit for military service, while others identify those who were not attending the services of the Established Church - Recusants Rolls, and Papists Lists. Other lists were for statistical purposes or curiosity; for example the Renhold census of 1773 {PO 13}, the Hinwick and Podington census of 1778 (in the British Library) and the Cardington census of 1782 {P38/28/1/1-2}. A detailed account by Chapman of pre-1841 censuses and population listings in Bedfordshire was published by the BHRS in 1993 [3]; for an account of listings throughout the British Isles see the publication by Lochin with a similar title [4].

None of the lists, made either for the decennial census returns or for other purposes, required the names to be in alphabetical order. Accordingly no indexes of names were prepared by the officials. But realising the value of the listings, Societies and individuals have transcribed and indexed (in varying quality) many of the returns. The 1881 census indexing was organised through the Federation of Family History Societies to a national standard and is undeniably the best. Some of the 1851 census indexes are of a similar quality. BFHS has indexed all of the 1851 census Bedfordshire returns. Some other listings for parts of Bedfordshire have been published by BHRS; for example, some 1297 Taxation Lists (vol 39), some Hearth Tax returns for 1671 (vol 16), the 1782 Census of Cardington (vol 52), some Land Transfers in southern Bedfordshire (1750-1832), particularly Aspley Guise and Tilsworth (vol 23), and some Muster Lists from 1539 to 1831 (vol 71) - although there are no comparable data to the 1777 Militia Listing for Northamptonshire. The CRO has copies of the available indexes to the decennial censuses and other population listings for Bedfordshire.

Maps

Having discovered an address for your ancestors in a Poll Book or Electoral register, found them in Directories and Gazetteers and located them in a Census or other Population Listing, it is helpful to study some maps to note nearby natural and man-made features and landmarks such as hills, rivers and other potential communication routes, and towns, villages, markets and mills that would have had an impact on your ancestors' lives. Some large scale maps have names of owners and tenants of properties, fields and dwellings so that you can gauge the extent of the holdings of your ancestors and their neighbours. Successive maps may indicate change in ownership or occupancy not noted in other records. An estate map often provides the earliest layout of a parish, although the most detailed are usually those prepared between 1775 and 1890 in connection with Parliamentary Inclosure or Tithe Commutation. Some maps have an accompanying schedule or reference book with details of owners and occupiers, landlords and tenants, rather than inscribing this information on the map itself.

The CRO holds an extensive collection of manuscript and printed maps relating to Bedfordshire from the 16th Century to the present; these are indexed by parish in the Map Index. BHRS has published a comprehensive catalogue (vol 62) of printed maps and town plans with their makers.

Property Records

The names of occupiers, as well as owners, are likely to appear in records associated with property and land, particularly when its value is being reassessed when a new landlord or tenant is anticipated. Thus deeds, terriers, surveys, maps (mentioned above), valuation lists, rentals, ratebooks and tax lists and even housing records can provide information on names of your ancestors, both owners and tenants, and the dates when they were living at specific addresses. An owner could be an individual or a corporate body such as a church, chapel, university, charity, trust or corporation. You are likely to discover additional details such as the value of the property, how much rent they paid and names of neighbours and the values of their properties, all of which are wonderful gems for any local, social or family historian. Land records associated with manors are mentioned in Chapter 4.

The CRO has many deeds and other property records stretching from 1188 to very recent times; its quarterly *Newsletters* in 1987-89 [5] have some useful articles on these records. The CRO catalogues of deeds contain names of parties and witnesses, with dates and details on the properties. Deeds are indexed by place in the main parish index. There are some glebe terriers (church property surveys) for 1607, 1708 and 1822 for all Bedfordshire parishes {ABE} and {FAC}. Valuations prepared as the basis for rate assessments for 1910 {DV} and 1925 {DBV} exist for the whole county. Many private estate records at the CRO contain rentals, terriers and surveys. Research in these can be complicated but the CRO Search Room staff are always willing to help and advise.

A particular type of property in which your ancestors may have had a interest, as an owner, tenant or customer is an inn or pub. The CRO has separate entries in its main index to inns and public houses {INN <place>/<sign>}.

Biographical Dictionaries and Who's Whos

If your ancestors were noteworthy in any field: writers, poets, military personnel, a mayor or Member of Parliament, a clergyman, doctor, surgeon, engineer, scientist, architect, or was a knight or Peer of the Realm, they are likely to appear in a specialist national directory or biographical dictionary, which were generally published annually or in many successive editions. In the majority of these publications the home address of the biographee is mentioned. Such national publications include *Who's Who*, first published in 1849, and *Who Was Who*, published from 1915; there was a *Cumulated Index for Who Was Who 1897-1980*. Other national directories and dictionaries include the (Anglican) *Crockford's Clerical Directory*, from 1858, the *Catholic Directory* from 1839, the *Medical Directory* from 1845, the *Dictionary of National Biography*, the

Army List, the *Navy List*, *Debrett's Peerage*, the *Complete Peerage* and *Burke's Commoners*. There were even some local biographies such as *Berks, Bucks & Bucks in the Twentieth Century: Contemporary Biographies* (1907), *The Bedford and Bedfordshire Who's Who and Year Book* (1909), and *Bedford and Bedfordshire Residential Guide* (1911), and *Who's Who in Bedfordshire and Huntingdonshire* (1936). Most of these biographical dictionaries are on the open shelves in the Search Room at the CRO. BCL and Luton Library have similar selections of biographical dictionaries and directories. The CRO has an unpublished listing of Bedfordshire clergy and their parishes (1200-1900) with an alphabetical index of names of clergy. You can gain ready access to considerably more unpublished and published material in the CRO, on lesser and greater county families, through the subject index under {FAMILIES<surname>}.

Migration

One of the challenges in genealogy is that our ancestors appear to be constantly on the move. They do not stay at the same address, particularly in towns in the 19th Century, although families were less likely to move than individuals searching for work or a spouse. The indexes and directories mentioned above will be helpful in locating individuals but you should consider possible migration causes and routes. In Bedfordshire the River Ouse, although only about three metres deep, was navigable from Bedford (from 1689) to The Wash and North Sea at Kings Lynn; the River Ivel was navigable from the Ouse at Tempsford to Shefford (from 1822), while the Grand Junction Canal (from 1805) followed the south western county boundary by Leighton Buzzard. Roads, some maintained by Turnpike Trusts, and railways (from 1838 and reaching Bedford on a branch line in 1846 and on a through route in 1857) were further possible migration routes your ancestors may have used. The Great North Road passed through the east of the county, and the Watling Street through the south west.

The CRO has records of some Turnpike Trusts (1706-1871). *The Railway Age in Bedfordshire* (BHRS vol 53) [6] is useful for information on rail routes. Although many people moved into towns such as Bedford, Dunstable and Luton, others did migrate from urban to rural areas for one reason or another. Others obviously moved out of the county, even overseas, searching for change and opportunity. Some assisted migration schemes in the 19th Century were often mentioned in Vestry Minutes (see Chapter 4). The names of people leaving the British Isles were not normally listed by officialdom and there are very few passenger lists at the PRO; however, there are likely to be lists of those arriving in the former colonies such as America, Canada, Australia, New Zealand and South Africa. Genealogical and family history societies (see final note on page 3) in these countries have indexed many such passenger arrivals.

Evidence of individuals or families legally migrating within the regulations of the Poor Laws may be found in Settlement Papers (see Chapter 4) at the CRO. BFHS and the CRO have jointly published an index [7] of personal names of surviving *Bedfordshire Poor Law Settlement Papers*. BFHS has also published *An Alphabetical List of Bedfordshire Strays* [8] identifying individuals and families "with Bedfordshire connections whose records have been found outside the county". As explained in Chapter 4, individuals and families who had migrated and become a financial burden on their adopted parish could be served a Removal Order, possibly after being questioned ("examined") by county magistrates at the Quarter Sessions, to return to their birth place, or place of legal settlement. Other ancestors may also have been compelled to migrate, being taken to a local or distant gaol pending a hearing or, as a result of a sentence even transported overseas if found guilty of a significant crime.

3. When Did Your Ancestors Live (and die) ?

Civil Registration

The national registration of births, marriages and deaths began (as mentioned on page 2) in 1837 for England and Wales. The whole country was divided into Registration Districts, co-terminous with the Poor Law Union areas established in 1834 under the New Poor Law (see page 34). Many areas fitted within county boundaries but occasionally spilled over into an adjacent county. For example, some of the Leighton Buzzard Union (and so the Leighton Buzzard Registration District) covered a part of Buckinghamshire, whilst part of the St Neots Union (in Huntingdonshire) included some Bedfordshire parishes. Other Registration Districts established in 1836 for the county were Ampthill, Bedford, Biggleswade, Luton and Woburn. The original Districts and subsequent changes for every parish in the county are detailed in Chapter 5. Woburn, as a Union and a Registration District, was dissolved on 26 September 1899 and its parishes absorbed into Ampthill and Leighton Buzzard Unions. The Bedfordshire parishes [9] originally in St Neots Union (and so Registration District) were transferred to the Bedford Registration District on 1 October 1935; those [10] in the Wellingborough Registration District were transferred on 1 July 1936. A new registration district of Dunstable was created on 1 April 1964 from parts [11] of Ampthill, Leighton Buzzard and Luton Registration Districts.

A birth, marriage or death was recorded by a local registrar who provided the informant with a certificate and sent a copy of the details via the Superintendent Registrar to the Registrar General in London, whose clerks every three months compiled national indexes of births, of marriages and of deaths. These indexes are available for free perusal at the Family Records Centre, Myddelton Place, London. Microform copies of the indexes are available locally (see page 2). A quarterly index entry has the name of the individual, the name of the Registration District in which the event was registered (not always when or where it took place) and a volume and page number of the entry in the Registrar General's files. For Bedfordshire all entries were in Volume 6 from 1837 to 1851, in Volume 3b from 1852 to March 1974, and in Volume 9 from the June quarter of 1974.

The local Registrars (see Chapter 7), to today, retain their original volumes, but having no search rooms, do not provide a public search facility. They hold only their own registers and use a totally different indexing system to that used at

Myddelton Place. As a result, whilst some Registrars are able to provide copies of certificates for their Registration Districts in response to postal applications, personal callers cannot be accommodated and the Myddelton Place reference numbers are of no use at all to them.

For other parts of the British Isles such as Scotland, Ireland, the Isle of Man and the Channel Islands, civil registration commenced after 1837, although in some instances was more comprehensive than in England and Wales. Information on civil registration systems throughout the British Isles is given in Chapman [12].

Copies of birth registrations (without the mothers' names) were sometimes held locally to enable the authorities in Poor Law Unions (and similar areas from 1927) to administer an effective vaccination programme and also to satisfy the requirements of the Education Acts at the end of the 19th Century. The CRO has birth registrations for vaccination purposes for the Ampthill Union (1873-1907) {PUAH 3/1-7}, the Bedford Union, rural areas (1881-83) {PUBV 15/1-3}, the Bedford area (1927-46) {GPV 36/1/1-20}, the Kempston, Cardington, Harrold and Riseley areas (1927-46) {GPV 36/2/1-20} and the Luton area (1891) {PULH 3/1}. The CRO also has birth registrations for education purposes for Bedford and Cardington (1897-1952) {EBV 3/1-2}, Bedford and Kempston (1897-1916) {EBV 3/3-4} and Bedford Borough (1916-37) {EBV 3/5-11}. The later Bedford Borough registrations are indexed {EBV 3/12-21}. The educational registration records also contain deaths of children in Bedford Borough (1897-1952) {EBV 4/1-4} with an index (1912-52) {EBV 4/5-6}.

Having used the civil registration birth and marriage certificates to 1837, and the 19th Century census returns to identify birthplaces, it should now be possible to turn to a parish where an individual was born. The parish and nonconformist registers of baptisms and marriages should be used (in the same manner as civil certificates of births and marriages) to work backwards generation by generation, possibly to 1538, assuming the family remained in the same parish; most of these registers, or copies of them, are now at the CRO, see the next four sections. If an individual cannot be found in the expected parish register, try looking in an adjacent or near-by parish, consider Nonconformity, Quaker, Roman Catholic or Jewish affiliation. The 1851 Ecclesiastical Census, of which very detailed abstracts were published by BHRS (vol 54), merits perusal as it describes all places of worship in the county for that year. Also remember migration (see Chapter 2). A map of Bedfordshire parishes, available from the CRO, will be very useful at this stage. In years gone by people walked much further than today to go about their daily lives. Nonconformists travelled quite long distances to to go about their daily lives. Nonconformists travelled quite long distances to attend services and some of their ministers carried one register book from chapel to chapel. Some parishes and incumbents, often in towns, attracted couples from surprisingly long distances, perhaps offering a fashionable or discount wedding. Marriages licence records (see below) may help at this stage. Many couples often met at a local market town, several just over the county boundary (see also page 26), so an old topographical map is also useful to identify pre-motorway routes. If the parish register has not survived researchers would usually be advised to look in the corresponding Bishop's Transcript (BT) - see below; but in the case of Bedfordshire, modern copies have been made of almost all of the registers and BTs and the entries generally integrated in the modern copies. It would normally be worth while looking in the BTs anyway, as some events can be found there which were never entered in an original register.

Parish (Anglican) Registers

Following the 16th Century Reformation in England and Wales, the regular recording of baptisms, marriages and burials in parish registers began in 1538, although not all parishes complied. Reminders to the clergy were issued in 1597 when it was also decreed that copies of the register entries should be made weekly and sent annually (usually on 25 March - New Year's Day until 1753) via the Archdeacon to the Bishop's Registrar in the Diocesan Registry. These contemporary copies have become known as Bishops' Transcripts (BTs). The Archdeacon of Bedford appears to have unusually retained the Transcripts in his own registry with only a few, apparently duplicate, Transcripts occasionally being passed to the Bishop of Lincoln.

Several Anglican Churches and Chapels were built to serve the needs of a particular congregation rather than a specific parish. These were called "non-parochial", as were any records or registers which they kept. The term was additionally applied to non-Anglican, e.g., Nonconformist, Quaker, Roman Catholic and Jewish material also having no Anglican parish commitment.

Several Bedfordshire parish registers commence in 1538. The years of the first entries in each parish register are given in Chapter 5. Most Bishops' (Archdeacons') Transcripts {ABT} for Bedfordshire survive from 1602 and are at the CRO. Most of the Bedfordshire parish registers are deposited at the CRO; a complete list of those held in the county archives, with dates covered by the baptismal, marriage and burial registers, is available for purchase from the CRO.

Other Ecclesiastical Records

Most people were married after the calling of banns in the parish churches where the man and woman lived. After Lord Hardwicke's Act of 1753, some marriage registers had a space to record that banns had been read and on which dates; in other cases, separate banns books were used. Some post-1753 banns books for Bedfordshire parishes, though generally with a gap from 1790 to 1823, are now at the CRO. It was also possible to be married after the issue of a common or ordinary licence by a bishop or an archbishop, or in extreme cases after the issue of a special licence from the Faculty Office of the Archbishop of Canterbury.

Associated with the issue of a common marriage licence were five documents: the Allegation or Affidavit also stating where the marriage could take place, the Bond, the Marriage Licence Register or Act Book, the Marriage Licence itself and the subsequent entry in the marriage register of the cathedral, parish church or chapel where the marriage took place. The CRO holds the Bonds (1747-1822) and Allegations or Affidavits for Bedford Archdeaconry (1578-1618, 1747-1885) {ABM}, and similar documents for the Peculiars of Biggleswade (1714-1860) {PB/M} and Leighton Buzzard (1792-1822) {RI 6820}. For an outline of the rights exercised by the Dukes of Bedford in the Woburn Peculiar see BHRS vol 49 pp 122-134. Some original Marriage Licences have survived among the individual parish records.

The Church, until the 19th Century, was responsible for many activities now undertaken by secular authorities. The issuing of a licence to practise as a schoolmaster or a surgeon or a midwife, the adjudicating on and punishment of sexual offences, and the granting of probate (see Chapter 4) are some of the activities in which Church officials became involved, often at a sitting of an Ecclesiastical Court. The records of these Church Courts also have references to misdemeanours of the clergy and the maintenance of ecclesiastical buildings, together with the appointment of lay officials as well as the clergy within the parishes. Because of the nature of many cases brought before the Church Courts they became known as the Bawdy Courts. For a full description of their operation and records see Chapman [13]. All the extant records of the Bedford Archdeacons' Courts {AB} are at the CRO. The original records of the Lincoln and Ely Diocesan Courts relating to Bedfordshire are at Lincoln [14] and Ely [15] respectively. The Hertfordshire CRO [16] also holds some St Albans Diocesan material relevant to Bedfordshire (post-1914), although by this time the Church Courts dealt only with ecclesiastical matters.

Register Copies & Indexes

The copying by hand of Bedfordshire parish registers, at least to 1812 and many integrated with available Bishops' Transcripts, was begun by F G Emmison in 1933. These were continued by the CRO and published, with indexes, in the *Bedfordshire Parish Registers Series* (*BPRS*) and are available on the open shelves at the CRO and for purchase from the CRO. They are also held in major libraries in the county and in London, and at some university libraries around the world. Many Bedfordshire parish registers from their commencement, generally to 1940 and in some cases to the 1980s, have also been microfilmed and fiches or other copies of selected parishes are available for purchase and in libraries in the county (for addesses see Chapter 7).

At the end of the 19th Century, William P W Phillimore an eminent genealogist, transcribed and published very many marriage registers to 1812 selected from all over the country. However, the only volume published by Phillimore relating to Bedfordshire was for Kensworth (1615-1812), in Hertfordshire at that time.

In the 1930s Percival Boyd studied and indexed hundreds of marriage registers throughout the country. Typescript copies of his indexes are deposited at the library of the Society of Genealogists. 8 of 127 ancient Bedfordshire parishes identified by Boyd [17] are included in *Boyd's Miscellaneous Series*.

Marriages in Bedfordshire parishes prior to 1812 not included on the IGI (see below) may be found in a card index at the CRO.

Indexed abstracts of Bedfordshire Marriage Allegations (1578-1618, 1747-1790 and 1791-1812), including those of Leighton Buzzard Peculiar, were published in *BPRS* Vols 14 and 15, identifying full names of the potential bridegrooms and brides. The CRO has typescript calendar of Bedford Archdeaconry allegations (1813-1885). A slip index for all Marriage Allegations (1813-49) is held by BFHS [18]. The Bonds and Allegations for Biggleswade Peculiar (1714-1800), these are not in *BPRS*, are catalogued at the CRO.

The CRO has computerised burial indexes for churches and chapels (not cemeteries - see page 24) for Bedford (1813-20th Century), Luton (1813-1904), Biggleswade Churchyard (1813-1942) and an amalgamated index for Potton, Sandy and Sutton (1813-20th Century). There are many other transcripts and indexes, held at the CRO in Bedford, prepared by volunteers and CRO staff, offering you ready access to original records.

Nonconformists, Quakers, Roman Catholics & Jews

Following the Reformation in England and Wales and until 1837 the only marriages recognised legally (apart from those of Quakers and Jews) were those performed by the Established (Anglican) Church. Thus everyone, even nonconformists, who sought a valid wedding had the service performed in a parish church following the calling of banns or issuing of a licence; the event was recorded in the parish marriage register, and as with Anglicans, normally that of the bride's residence. Quakers and Jews were permitted to conduct their own services and maintain their own registers.

From 1837 nonconformist meeting houses could be licensed for marriages and so began their own registers. Even before this some nonconformists performed their own baptisms and infant dedication ceremonies; some had their own burial grounds and conducted their own burial services, and some registers associated with these services were maintained. Practising Roman Catholicism was forbidden after the Reformation until 1791 when the building of public chapels for Roman Catholic worship was permitted; the 1829 Emancipation Act further encouraged their expansion. Accordingly there are few ancient Roman Catholic records. There are, however, Lists of Papists and Recusants Rolls which were compiled nationally in the seventeenth and eighteenth centuries. The whereabouts of this material is given in Chapman [19]. Jews were permitted to settle in England from 1658, having been banished in 1290.

Nonconformity was particularly strong in Bedfordshire but there were very few Roman Catholic and Jewish communities until the 20th Century. Independent, Baptist, Congregational, Moravian, Methodist (Wesleyan, Primitive and others) and Quaker congregations met from the 17th Century, building Chapels and Meeting Houses across the county and maintaining their "non-parochial" registers and records. An outline of Recusancy and Nonconformity in the county (1622-1842) was published by BHRS (vol 20).

In 1840 and again in 1858 the Registrar General requested that nonconformists and others deposit their "non-parochial" registers. Not all congregations obliged; but the registers of those who did are now in the Public Record Office, London, in the RG4 to RG6 series, where they may be consulted; the CRO has microfilm copies {MIC 150-152} of the non-parochial registers relating to Bedfordshire; all have been transcribed and indexed. No Roman Catholic congregations surrendered their registers to the Registrar General. In recent years further nonconformist and some Roman Catholic material for Bedfordshire has been deposited directly at the CRO.

The first nonconformists to make an impact in Bedfordshire were the Independents (usually becoming Congregationalists, now the United Reformed Church) and then the Baptists. The records of Bunyan Meeting, Bedford, Independent Chapel {BY} begin in 1656. Congregational records at the CRO are those of Howard Chapel Bedford (1777-1965) {X 420}, Dunstable (1854-1920 {X 855}, Harrold (1812-36) {MIC 151}, Hockliffe & Eggington (1809-1925) {X 270}, Roxton (1824-37) {MIC 152}, Shillington (1827-1993) {X 846}, Turvey (1828-72) {X 729}. The earliest Baptist records (1672) in the county held at the CRO are of Stevington Chapel (1672-1883) {X 239}. Other Baptist records (some in microform or only transcripts) at the CRO which include church books, lists of members, registers of births and burials, and monumental inscriptions, are of Bedford Mill Street (1792-1836) {MIC 150}, Biggleswade (1771-1962) {X 350}, Blunham (1724-1893) {X 525}, Cardington Cotton End (1776-1889) {X 358}, Carlton (1688-1854) {170}, Cranfield (1794-1837) {MIC 152}, Heath & Reach (1822-1960) {X 305}, Houghton Regis (1772-1836) {MIC 152}, Kensworth 1675-1811) {170}, Keysoe Brook End {X 715}, Keysoe Row (1812-1967) {X 629}, Leighton Buzzard, Lake Street (1771-1939) {X 648}, Luton Limbury (1911-68) {X 626}, Luton Park Street (1777-1837) {MIC 171}, Maulden (1768-1854) {MIC 112}, Ridgmont (1701-1951) {X 347}, Riseley (1838-1867) {170}, Sharnbrook (1719-1838) {170}, Sharnbrook Bethlehem Chapel (1833-1907) {170}, Shefford Hardwick (1832-36) {MIC 152}, Southill (1693-1837) {170/4/5 & MIC 152}, Little Staughton (1771-1849) {X 187}, Thurleigh (1837-1978) {X 349}, Toddington (1816-1953) {Micf 55}, Westoning (1810-36) {MIC 152} and Wootton {X 834}.

Wesleyan Methodists were very active in Bedfordshire and had circuits based on Ampthill, Bedford, Biggleswade, Dunstable, Leighton Buzzard and Luton, all of whose records {MB} including registers, class lists (of members) and minutes of business meetings, are in the CRO. The first Methodist Church Book (1781-1806) which covers Bedfordshire and surrounding counties has been transcribed and is available for purchase from the CRO. The earliest Methodist Chapel registers in the CRO are of Eaton Bray (from 1798) {MIC 152} and Biggleswade (from 1799) {MIC 150}. Some Bedfordshire chapels were served by circuits outside the county, e.g. St Neots (records at the CRO), Bletchley and Wolverton (records at Buckinghamshire RO), Hitchin and Harpenden (records at Hertfordshire RO), and Higham Ferrers (records at Northamptonshire RO). Methodism suffered a number of divisions during the 19th Century, into the

Methodist New Connection (1797), Primitive Methodists (1811), Bible
Christians (1819), Protestant Methodists (1829), the Wesleyan Methodist
Association (1836) and Reformers (1849); there was some reconciliation into the
United Methodist Free Churches in 1856, the United Methodist Church in 1907
and The Methodist Church in 1932, leaving the Independent Methodists and the
Wesleyan Reform Union as separate bodies with their own archives. Besides
those mentioned above, the CRO has many original archives {MB-} and has
microfilm copies {MIC & Micf} of nearly 40 Methodist Chapels in Bedfordshire
and has a computer-generated index to baptisms in local circuits. The CRO holds
copies of records of Methodist congregations from adjoining counties where
Bedfordshire individuals and families were members, enjoying the services.

Moravians should not be overlooked in this county, with churches in Bedford and
Risely. Moravian archives {MO} at the CRO include catalogues of the Bedford
congregation (1744-1871) and monumental inscriptions from burial grounds in
Bedford {CRT 120/15} and their Pertenhall Chapel (1831-1960) {CRT 170/7/5}.

The register of the Bedford Primitive Episcopal Church {Z 273/1} for baptisms
and burials (1832-1845) is at the CRO.

During the 17th Century, eighteen Society of Friends (Quaker) Meetings were
established in Bedfordshire; the CRO has digests {FR} of Quaker births,
marriages and burials in the county from this time and also microform copies
{MIC 34-37 & 51-53} of records relating to Bedfordshire Quakers deposited with
the Registrar General. A photocopy of the Buckinghamshire Quaker Marriage
Register (1658-1835) is in the Search Room, and there is a list {CRT 170/5/16} of
Quaker births, marriages and deaths (1663-1955) in the Berkhamstead area.

The proportion of Catholics in Bedfordshire to the total population in 1676 was
one of the lowest in the Province of Canterbury. The first recorded Catholic
Mission established in the county after the Reformation was in 1728 at Shefford,
but this declined. Roman Catholic dioceses were re-established in England in
1850; Northampton was chosen as the Cathedral Parish for the Catholic Diocese
of Northampton comprising the counties of Bedford, Buckingham, Cambridge,
Huntingdon, Norfolk, Northampton and Suffolk. The Shefford congregation was
re-established by 1851, St Francis' Church was opened in 1884 and its registers,
on microfilm {MIC 199} at the CRO, begin in 1885. St Joseph's Roman Catholic
Church was opened in Bedford in 1863; its registers commence in 1864 {MIC
226}. The only other Catholic communities established in the county prior to the
20th Century were at Campton (1851), Leighton Buzzard (1895) and Luton

(1884). It should be remembered that in any case Roman Catholics were not permitted to marry other than in the Established Anglican Church until after 1836; hence their marriages before this date should be found in parish registers.

No Jewish community appeared in Bedfordshire for many years. The activities of the small Jewish community in Bedford and its Synagogue from 1803-27 and from 1837 have been extensively researched by Patricia Bell [20] from records {HT} of the Bedford Charity (Harpur Trust) at the CRO and from other archives. A Hebrew Congregation in Luton was consecrated at Moor Park in 1925.

International Genealogical Index (IGI)

The Genealogical Society of Utah (GSU) has been undertaking a world-wide project for many years to film and transcribe baptismal and marriage registers of all denominations. From the transcriptions, county alphabetical indexes have been published thus providing a wonderful finding aid for researchers. Indexes for English and Welsh counties were first produced in 1976 on microfiche as the Computer File Index (CFI). Published materials, such as Emmison's transcripts were also incorporated into the GSU index. When republished in 1980 it was renamed the International Genealogical Index (IGI), mentioned on page 8 above. As the IGI shows only a minimum of data culled from several sources, including personal documents, it must be used only as an index to the original records which should be consulted wherever possible. Most Bedfordshire parish registers have been filmed by the GSU and so the IGI coverage for the county is good. Accordingly, you should not neglect this extremely useful finding aid, now available on CD-ROM and microfiche. The CRO and several libraries in the county hold the 1992 microfiche edition of the IGI.

Memorial Inscriptions

Memorial inscriptions (MIs) on gravestones, tombstones, monumental brasses, church furnishings and bells at parish churches, and burial grounds and meeting houses of other denominations, often provide details on individuals not found in registers or elsewhere. Local and family historians have copied and indexed a number of the inscriptions on Bedfordshire memorials. A Weight Matthews, an amateur local historian, travelled throughout the county in the early 20th Century transcribing monumental inscriptions from church and chapel graveyards [21] into notebooks which he entitled *Ye Old Mortality*. His books are at the Society of Genealogists, London, but photocopies {CRT 120/15} are held at the CRO. The transcriptions of Col Chester from many other parishes and of L H Chambers (who recorded 22 graveyards 1915-45), and of other individuals and groups, are in the CRO, also under {CRT 120/15}. A list is available at the CRO of surveys that have been undertaken. There are several indexed books on Bedfordshire monumental brasses at the CRO, BCL and libraries throughout the county.

Cemeteries

Cemeteries are grounds, other than church or chapel yards, set aside for burial of the dead. By the early 19th Century parish churchyards, particularly in towns, had become so full that the inadequate burial of corpses was causing not only congestion but serious health problems from the spread of diseases. As a result both private and public cemeteries were opened, the first being in Norwich in 1819. A Cemetery Clauses Act of 1847, a Public Health Act of 1848 (spurred on by dreadful outbreaks of cholera in 1846 and 1848) and a series of Burial Acts from 1850 to 1857 enabled a short-lived General Board of Health and then the Local Government Board to empower private companies and parish Burial Boards in urban and rural areas to open cemeteries. These were usually divided into consecrated and unconsecrated areas with often two or more chapels for burial services by Anglicans and Nonconformists and, later, Roman Catholics.

Examples in Bedfordshire are the Bedford Joint Burial Board set up in 1853, opening Bedford Cemetery in 1855, and the Luton Cemetery Company opening two cemeteries in 1854, one in Rothsay Road and one in Crawley Road. Other burial boards were established in the county and opened cemeteries at Campton & Shefford (1854), Toddington (1856), Dunstable (1861), Biggleswade (1867), Turvey (1871), Kempston (1877), Potton (1880), Flitton (1881), Leighton Buzzard (1882), Cople (1883), Eaton Bray (1883), Caddington (1885) and Sandy (1889). From 1895 the responsibility for cemeteries was passed to parish or town councils. Cemeteries established by parish councils include Stotfold (1897), Harlington (1889), Blunham (1902), Wootton (1922), Heath & Recah (1926), Eaton Socon (1930), Harrold (1939), Wymington (1942), Flitwick (1951). Cemetery records normally include the locations of graves, names of grave purchasers and dates of purchase, besides the names of the persons buried, the date of burial and, sometimes, also the date of death. For cemeteries in Bedfordshire these records are mostly now with the local councils which have assumed responsibility for the cemeteries from the Burial Boards although the CRO holds the registers for Kempston, Potton and Toddington. The CRO has microfilm copies of the cemetery records for Bedford, Biggleswade, Blunham, Cople, Dunstable, Eaton Bray, Leighton Buzzard, Luton (two grounds), Sandy and Stotfold.

4. How Did Your Ancestors Live ?

Trades, Occupations and Professions

A few enthusiastic historians and organisations are compiling national and local indexes of individuals involved in particular trades and occupations. The CRO has indexes of professions including architects, artists, clergy, lawyers and solicitors and their clerks, magistrates, medical men, photographers, surveyors and other occupations, within the subject index. Bedfordshire Clock and Watchmakers were the subject of BHRS volume 70. An index of canal and river boatmen and allied trades working on inland waterways is held by Mr J Roberts of Sutton Coldfield [22]. Occupations mentioned in Bedfordshire wills are on a card index in the CRO. Trades Directories and Biographical Dictionaries (see Chapter 2) provide details of the more affluent traders and professionals in the county. Many archives of former Bedfordshire businesses and private and institutional employers have been deposited at the CRO; BHRS published a volume (60) on agricultural labour based on 19th Century records in the CRO and PRO. Archives of the Lucas family of central Bedfordshire, the collection of the Luton solicitor Austin, and the records of the County (Lunatic) Asylum are just three examples from hundreds of deposits where you may find an ancestor or two as an employee (or even an employer).

Prior to becoming a recognised craftsman, tradesman or professional, most people underwent training or an apprenticeship. Formal apprenticeship involved the youth's father or guardian agreeing for the child to serve a Master craftsman or tradesman for a fixed term, usually seven years. The agreement, which included the name, address and trade of the Master, the name and address of the father and name of the apprentice, was drawn up on parchment or paper and often cut into two portions (one for each party) with a wavy or indented line and hence the document was termed an indenture. Orphans, particularly pauper children dependent on parish relief, might be apprenticed by the parish overseers to a Master in another, sometimes distant parish. Central government raised cash from 1710-1811 by taxing Apprenticeship Indentures; these records are in the PRO, London, in the Inland Revenue (IR1) series. The CRO holds a number of original Apprenticeship Indentures including parish pauper apprenticeships {P<parish number>/14}, the Harpur Trust (Bedford Charity) apprenticeship registers (1761-1814 and 1840-41) {X109/1, X171/62 and HT8} and a typescript calendar of apprenticeship registers for Bedford Borough (1615-1843). There is also a list of Bedfordshire apprentices (1711-1720) in BHRS vol 9, and a small manuscript index at the CRO of Bedfordshire Masters and their Apprentices, taken from holdings in the Society of Genealogists' library.

Newspapers

Increasingly in the 19th Century, newspapers reported a variety of social events as well as other news items. The first paper circulating throughout Bedfordshire was the *Northampton Mercury* established in 1720. Notices of births, marriages and deaths, obituaries and reports on funerals, on court cases and other Bedfordshire events were included even after the county's own specific newspapers began in 1837 and 1845. The *Cambridge Chronicle*, from 1762, also contains Bedfordshire material. The *Huntingdon, Bedford and Peterborough Weekly Gazette* was founded in 1813. The *Bedford Mercury and Huntingdon Express* began in 1837 and the *Bedford Times* in 1845. Other newspapers in the county were the *Luton Record* (1855), the *Luton Times* (1855), the *Dunstable Chronicle* (1856), the *Leighton Buzzard Observer and Linslade Gazette* (1861), the *Ampthill and District News* (1891) and the *Biggleswade Chronicle and Sandy, Potton and Shefford Times* (1891). The CRO has a collection of some of these and many other local newspapers with some indexes; for example the *Bedfordshire Times* (1845-1970) index {BP 43/1-13}, whilst extracts from the local news columns (1860-95) of the *Bedfordshire Mercury* are included in the CRO main parish index. BCL has a comprehensive collection of local newspapers in hard copy and on microfilm. Luton Library and Luton Museum have some of the south Bedfordshire papers. Conisbee has a useful list of relevant county newspapers and periodicals in Section A16.

Markets and Fairs

If your ancestors were involved in any form of trading - buying or selling, agricultural products or livestock - this would have been undertaken at one or more of the weekly or bi-weekly markets held all over the country. Much larger trading fairs were also held in some towns several times a year and at which entertainment was often provided; some fairs were for hiring seasonal or more permanent workers, whereas towards the end of the 19th Century others were entirely for pleasure. Some markets and fairs were established by Royal Charters and are of very ancient origin. Many, but certainly not all, were held on the patronal festival day of the dedication of the parish church. As many couples, possibly your ancestors, first met at a market or fair, an appreciation of

Bedfordshire and neighbouring market towns and the days on which the markets and fairs flourished is helpful in tracing their movements. The market towns can be located on old maps, e.g., Saxton (1576), Speed (1601) and Bowen (1760) (see Chapter 2); but the mediaeval origins of many of the county's fairs was given by Godber [23], taken from the *VCH*. The CRO card subject index has a section {TRADE & INDUSTRY Fairs and markets <place>}. The following list is derived from Lysons (1813) [24] and Lewis (1831) [25] but the popularity of markets and fairs rose and fell as the 19th Century progressed and several traditional market days and dates of annual fairs were changed. By the First World War many markets and fairs had ceased altogether; by 1931 the nature of the weekly market had changed and annual fairs were held only in Ampthill, Bedford, Biggleswade, Dunstable, Leighton Buzzard, Luton, Potton, Silsoe and Toddington.

Ampthill: Market day Thursday.
Annual statute fair on 29 September; annual cattle fairs on 4 May and 30 November.

Aspley Guise: Market day Friday (ceased before 1813).
Annual fair on St Botolph's Day (17 June) (ceased before 1831).

Bedford: Market day Monday for cattle, Saturday for corn and provisions (changed in mid-19th Century to Saturday for cattle and general purposes). Annual cattle fairs on first Tuesday in Lent, 21 April, 5 July, 21 August, 12 October and 19 December; wool fair on 17 November (changed in mid-19th Century to pleasure fairs on 21 & 22 April and 12 & 13 October; wool fairs on first Tuesday in July).

Biggleswade: Market day Wednesday for corn (also Monday for stock introduced in mid-19th Century).
Annual horse and live stock fairs on 13 February, Saturday in Easter week, Whit Monday, 2 August, and 8 November (changed in mid-19th Century to only 14 February).

Blunham: Market day Wednesday (ceased before 1813).
Annual fair on St James Day (25 July) (ceased before 1831).

Dunstable: Market day Wednesday for corn, cattle and garden produce.
Annual sheep fairs on Ash Wednesday, 22 May, 12 August, 12 November.

Elstow: Annual cattle fairs on 14 & 15 May and 5 & 6 November.

Harrold: Market day Thursday (failing by 1813; revived and moved to Tuesday by 1831; ceased in 1880).
Annual cattle and pedlary fairs on Tuesdays preceding 13 May, 6 July, 11 October.

Ickleford: Annual fair on 2 August.

Leighton Buzzard: Market day Tuesday for cattle, corn (toll free), lace, straw plait, provisions and other merchandise; (from mid-19th Century also Saturday for meat, fish and vegetables).
Annual horse and cattle fairs on 5 February, second Tuesday in April, Whit Tuesday, 26 July, 24 October and second Tuesday in December; (from mid-19th Century changed to Tuesday following 5 February, last Tuesday in April, Whit Tuesday, Tuesday following 26 July, 24 October, 10 December; a wool fair on first Friday in July, and an additional statute fair on Tuesday following 11 October).

Luton: Market day Monday for cattle, corn and straw plait; (from mid-19th Century also Saturday for provisions).
Annual statute fair in September, cattle fairs on 18 April, 18 October; (from mid-19th Century on third Mondays in April and October).

Odell: Market day Thursday (ceased long before 1813).
Annual fair on Thursday and Friday in Whitsun week.

Potton: Market day Saturday for corn, straw plait etc.
Annual horse and sheep fairs on third Tuesday in January, last Tuesday in April, first Tuesday in July, Tuesday before 29 October; (changed in mid-19th Century to last Monday in January or first Tuesday in February). Annual statute fair for hiring servants three weeks prior to Old Michaelmas Day (11 October).

Shefford: Market day Friday (ceased shortly before 1813).
Annual cattle and sheep fairs on 23 January, Easter Monday, 19 May; for pleasure on 10 October; (the cattle and sheep fairs had ceased by 1831 and the pleasure fair moved to 11 October).

Silsoe: Market day Tuesday (ceased long before 1813).
Annual fairs on 13 May and 21 September; (the September fair ceased during the 19th Century).

Sundon: Market day Friday and fair (ceased before 1813).

Toddington: Market day Saturday.
Annual fairs on 23 April, first Monday in June, 24 September, 16 December; (changed in mid-19th Century to 25 April and first Wednesday in October).

Old Warden: Market day Tuesday (ceased before 1813).
Annual fair on 29 June (ceased before 1813).

Woburn: Market day Friday.
Annual fairs on 1 January, 23 March (especially for horses), 13 July and 6 Oct.

[Markets and Fairs in neighbouring counties at which Bedfordshire people were regular participants]

Baldock (Hrt): Market day Friday for straw plait; (prior to 1830 was a general market on Saturday).
Annual cheese and horse fairs on 7 March, last Thursday in May, 5 August, 2 October and 11 December.

Gamlingay (Cam): Market ceased by 1831 in favour of Potton.

Harpenden (Hrt): Annual horse and cattle fair on 16 May.

Hemel Hempstead (Hrt): Market day Thursday for corn, straw plait and general purposes.
Annual sheep, cattle and pleasure fairs on Thursday after Trinity Sunday; annual statute fair for hiring servants on third Monday in September.

Higham Ferrers (Nth): Former market day Saturday but reinstated about 1900 on a Monday.
Annual fairs on Tuesday before 5 February, 6 March, Thursday before Old May Day (12 May), 28 June, Thursday before 5 August, 11 October; annual cattle fair on 6 December.

Hitchin (Hrt): Market day Tuesday, privately organised in 1931: by Geo Jackson in the Cock Inn yard for fat and store stock, horses, carriages and farming implements; by Page & Harding of St Albans in Queen Street for cattle etc.
Annual pleasure fairs on Easter and Whit Tuesdays and Wednesdays.

Kimbolton (Hun): Market day Friday.
Annual toy fairs on Friday in Easter week, Friday in Whitsun week, Friday after Old Michaelmas Day (11 October); annual ("Tandry") fair on Old St Andrew's Day (11 December); annual statute fair for hiring servants on the nearest Wednesday to 21 September.

Newport Pagnell (Bkm): Market day Saturday; (changed to Wednesday in mid-19th Century).
Annual fairs on 22 February, 22 April, 22 June, 29 August, 22 October and 22 December (limited to only 22 June in mid-19th Century).

Olney (Bkm): Market day Thursday.
Annual fairs on Easter Monday and 13 October; "Cherry" fair on 29/30 June.

Royston (Hrt): Market day Wednesday for corn, sheep, pigs and straw plait.
Annual fairs on Ash Wednesday, Easter Wednesday, Whit Wednesday, first Wednesday in July, first Wednesday after 10 Oct. for hiring servants and cattle.

St Albans (Hrt): Market day Saturday for corn, straw plait and provisions.
Annual cattle and horse fairs on 25 and 26 March; annual statute fairs on 10, 11 12 October; (changed in mid-19th Century to 25 March and 10 October for cows, horses, pigs and sheep, with annual toy fairs on 11 and 12 October).

St Neots (Hun): Market day Thursday for corn (and from mid-19th Century also for fat and store cattle sales).
Annual fairs on Ascension Day, on that day three weeks later and 17 December; annual statute fair for hiring servants on 1 August; (changed in mid-19th Century to a Thursday at the end of September).

Stony Stratford (Bkm): Market day Friday.
Annual fair on Friday after 10 October; annual cattle fairs on 2 August and 12 November.

Tring (Hrt): Market day Friday for corn, meat, pedlary and straw plait.
Annual fairs on Easter Monday and Old Michaelmas Day (11 October).

Wellingborough (Nth): Market day Wednesday.
Annual cattle fair on Wednesday in Easter week; annual pleasure fair on Wednesday in Whitsun week; annual sheep and cattle fair on 29 October.

Educational Establishments

Education in the British Isles was promoted by the Church from the 7th Century when schools (still existing today) were established in Canterbury, Rochester and York. The universities of Oxford and Cambridge were founded in the 12th Century. Prior to the Reformation, monasteries and nunneries respectively offered education for boys and girls. In very many villages the parish priest held a school, usually in the church, often over the south porch or in the tower. After the Reformation and Civil War, and religious toleration gained favour, dissenters established their own schools and academies for their adherents and their children. From the 15th Century schools were founded and endowed by wealthy merchants to teach the skills of reading, writing and arithmetic to potential recruits (irrespective of denominational loyalty) to their expanding businesses as international trade developed alongside world exploration. Many such schools evolved into grammar and public schools whose records, in many cases, stretch from their foundation to the present. The endowed Harpur Trust schools in Bedford have been unique in bringing families to the town over many generations, specifically to educate their children.

Charity schools were established from the end of the 17th Century which enabled even the poorest children to be provided not only with education but clothing, food and boarding. Many of these "hospital schools", funded by bodies like SPCK, had such distinctive clothing that they were termed Blue Coat, Green, Yellow or Red Coat Schools, as appropriate. Military schools offered education for children of soldiers and sailors and even civilians who worked at related establishments such as dockyards. From the early 19th Century National Schools (using the ideas of Bell, an Anglican clergyman) and British Schools (using similar ideas of Lancaster, a Quaker) spread throughout the country. Village Schools, Dame Schools and private institutions, Reformatory Schools for boys and girls and adult schools were opened as the 19th Century progressed. By the First World War there was a school in every or a nearby parish. Bushby's *Bedfordshire Schoolchild* (BHRS Vol 67) details many early schools in the county and the provision available at specific periods. Private schools such as the Bedford Middle Class School (see BHRS Vol 72), the Knolls at Woburn Sands and the Lidlington Academy provided education in the county. The Bedford Blue Coat School, founded in 1760, was later united with the National School.

Many schools kept admissions registers and log books, management, governors or board minutes, awards and punishment books with records of teachers and pupils. In some cases the funding body has the documentation today, in other cases the records are still at the school. The CRO has records of some Bedfordshire schools {SD} in all of the above categories indexed under {EDUCATION Schools <place>}, the Meppershall Charity School pupil records from 1690, for example. Records at the CRO of Carlton Reformatory from 1851 {X 521}, the Bedfordshire Training Home for Girls (1879-1931) {ST 1497-1545}, St Francis Roman Catholic Boys' Home, Shefford (1870-1967) {X 455/1-10} are among those of institutions for children not in the care of their parents. A very useful *Conspectus of State Education Records in Bedfordshire County Record Office*, listing which of the records identified above have survived and for which dates, is available at the CRO. Some of the older schools founded in the county are at Bedford (1552), Biggleswade (1557), Dunstable (1100) (but Chews School in 1727), Houghton Conquest (1632), Houghton Regis (1564) and Tempsford (1517). The Society of Genealogists has an extensive collection of school registers in its London library. The records of the Harpur Trust {HT} in the CRO include many details on its schools and other interests in Bedford.

The names of students at Oxford and Cambridge Universities have been recorded in *Alumni Oxoniensis* and *Alumni Cantabrigiensis*, available in most large reference libraries. Considerably more detail on the growth of British education, and its records of particular use to family historians, is given in the Chapmans Records Cameo on Education [26].

Probate

You may be able to discover a great deal on how your ancestors lived, their occupations, the crops they grew, the sizes of their homes, descriptions of their worldly possessions and an indication of their wealth, social status and friends from probate material - their wills, inventories, or Letters of Administration (Admons), if they died intestate.

The Established Church was responsible for probate - proving wills and granting Admons until 1858. The Ecclesiastical Court in which probate was granted depended on where the deceased lived or died and owned property, and the value of the estate. Details on the range of ecclesiastical courts and of procedures followed in them are described in Chapman's *Ecclesiastical Courts, Their Officials and Their Records* [27]. As described on page 6, Bedfordshire is in the Archdeaconry of Bedford, was successively in the Dioceses of Lincoln, Ely and St Albans, and is in the Province of Canterbury. The Lincoln Consistory Court delegated its testamentary powers in Bedfordshire to the Archdeacon's Court; hence even probate which would normally be granted in a bishop's court was dealt with by the Archdeacon of Bedford. Accordingly Bedfordshire wills are likely to have been proved in the Court of the Archdeacon of Bedford or possibly in the Prerogative Court of the Archbishop of Canterbury (PCC), and rarely in the Consistory Courts of the Bishop of Lincoln or of the Bishop of Ely. A comprehensive explanation of the Probate Courts which operated for Bedfordshire testators is given by Chris Pickford in the British Record Society (BRS) annual publication for 1993 (vol 104), *Index of Bedfordshire Probate Records 1484-1858.*

The original Bedford Archdeaconry Probate Court records (wills 1480-1858) {ABP/W}, Letters of Administration (1670-1858) {ABP/AR} and a few surviving inventories {ABP 4/} are at the CRO. Probate material {PBwP} from the Biggleswade (1720-1858) and the Leighton Buzzard (1701-1858) Peculiar Courts {PLBP} is also at the CRO; the Woburn Peculiar did not deal with probate so this was handled in the Bedford Archdeaconry Probate Court. The PCC probate material is held at the PRO, London, although photocopies of Bedfordshire wills proved in the PCC to 1700 are in the CRO {FAC 1 PROB 11}. The CRO has a card index (name, place and trade) to testators of the wills proved in the Bedford Archdeacons' and the Peculiar Courts. BRS (in vols 104 & 105) has published and indexed names of the testators of the probate material (1484-1858) held at the CRO. Indexes to Wills and Admons from the PCC from 1383 have also been published by the BRS [28], as have indexes to probate records (1449-1858) for the Ely Consistory Court (in vols 106-108). Abstracts from the Archdeaconry records 1480-1528 have been published by BHRS (vols 37 and 45), indexed by names of persons and places, as have abstracts of wills proved in the PCC from 1383 to 1548 (vol 58). In 1890 F A Blaydes published abstracts of many Bedfordshire wills (1538-1700) in his parochially arranged *Genealogia Bedfordiensis* [29]; he produced a typescript supplement in 1909, now held by the Society of Genealogists. 166 Bedfordshire inventories between 1617 and 1619 were indexed and published by BHRS (vol 20) and 15 earlier ones (1562-91) in BHRS (vol 32). The volumes cited above are available on the open shelves in the Search Room at the CRO and in some large public reference libraries.

In 1858 the Ecclesiastical Probate Courts were closed and civil Probate Courts and registries were opened; copies of the granted probate were sent to the Principal Probate Registry, Family Division, now at Somerset House, London

[30], indexed alphabetically in annual volumes for the whole of England and Wales. These may be consulted free of charge in London and copies of the probate documents purchased for a modest fee. Bedfordshire did not have its own (civil) Probate Registry and most wills were proved in the Northampton Court of Probate and (civil) Registry, although there was no restriction on where they could be proved. The Northamptonshire Record Office [31] holds copies of wills (1858-1930) proved, and grants of administration (1858-62) in the Northampton (civil) Probate Court. The original documentation relating to the Northampton Court is at the Birmingham District Probate Registry [32]. The Bedfordshire CRO has copies on microfiche {Micf 122} of the published Probate Calendars for all of England and Wales from 1858 to 1943.

You may also find copies of wills and other probate material associated with deeds, solicitors' archives and family papers. The CRO has a card index of "stray" wills deposited within these collections, also including copies of wills proved outside Bedfordshire.

The Old and New Poor Laws

Social security has been available in one form or another in England and Wales for over a thousand years. Originally provided by the Monarch, and also with shelter, food and clothing being available in mediaeval monasteries and abbeys, it became administered locally but somewhat loosely from the 15th Century. A series of Poor Laws in the 16th and 17th Centuries tightened up who was entitled to relief and under what conditions. Being born in a parish or working there or serving as a parish officer gave some entitlement, but the rules were modified on several occasions. Living or working in a parish for a year were generally suitable qualifications for eligibility for relief; but the many disputes regarding entitlement and cases of removing paupers to their birthplaces (or places of legal settlement), were brought before the local magistrates at the Quarter Sessions. Dubious cases were examined, illegally settled persons ordered to be removed and fathers of illegitimate children were ordered to pay towards their upkeep. An unmarried mother was required to name the father of her bastard child and a warrant was issued for his arrest if his ready support was not forthcoming. Illegitimate children were taught skills through parochially-organised apprenticeships (see above) in an attempt to reduce the potential drain on parish funds brought about by unskilled, unemployable residents entitled to relief. The dole was distributed from parochially collected funds by Overseers of the Poor elected annually at a meeting of the Parish Vestry.

Workhouses, providing in-door relief, began to be built for the infirm poor in the 18th Century, but the whole social security system became so thoroughly corrupt and expensive that a New Poor Law was introduced in 1834. The administration was vested in Guardians of the Poor responsible for Poor Law Union areas - each named after the location of its workhouse. The Unions to which each Bedfordshire parish was assigned are given in Chapter 5. Lying-in rooms in the workhouses later developed into hospitals.

Some of the administration of the Old Poor Laws thus fell on the shoulders of county magistrates and was dealt with at Quarter Sessions, whilst parish overseers, churchwardens and constables also became involved in their regular implementation. The New Poor Laws additionally involved the Guardians. The documentation associated with the Old and New Poor Laws is, therefore, dispersed in several different files in archives across the country. The Bedfordshire CRO, in parish {P<parish name>/11-18} and quarter sessions {QS} and other records in connection with the Old Poor Laws, has many settlement certificates, examination papers, removal orders, bastardy bonds, warrants for arrests of erring fathers, apprenticeship indentures, overseers' accounts and constables' accounts and notebooks. In the Poor Law Union archives {PU} from 1834, the CRO has Poor Law Guardians' minutes, numerous ledgers, vouchers, receipt and account books, outdoor relief books, admission and discharge books, birth and death registers, day books and journals, visitors' books, medical reports and hospital records, and mounds of correspondence relating to the social security in Bedfordshire until 1929, when central and local government took over the entire system. There is a card index in the CRO Search Room of names associated with the Poor Laws taken mainly from post-1834 records of the Quarter and Petty Sessions, Poor Law Union documentation and stray settlement cases. The CRO with BFHS has published [33] an index of names from all the surviving Parish Settlement Papers from 1622 to 1834.

In addition to the Poor Law records held at the CRO, there are vast amounts of documentation at the PRO in the MH series. In MH12 alone there are over 16,000 volumes of correspondence between the local Guardians and the Poor Law Commission to 1847 and the Poor Law Board after that. The Bedfordshire material from 1834 to 1900 is arranged by Unions in MH12/1-138; later correspondence which survived destruction during the Second World War is in MH68. There is some interesting correspondence between 1837 and 1876 in MH19/22 regarding emigration of paupers. MH9 and MH19 have information on various officers appointed in each Union from 1837 to 1921, while MH27 deals with schooling for the poor from 1848 to 1910. Do not forget that some Bedfordshire parishes on the county boundary fell into Unions associated with other counties and so their New Poor Law records are likely to be found there.

Parish and Borough Records

The parish church registers of baptism, marriage and burial have been described in Chapter 3; the parish as an administrative unit for collecting and distributing poor law relief by overseers appointed at a Vestry Meeting was mentioned in the previous section. The parish, as both an ecclesiastical and a secular entity, and the borough in urban areas, influenced almost every aspect of the lives of your ancestors, creating many records now in the CRO that can be used today to discover more about them. The decisions taken at meetings of the Vestry (originally all the parishioners and later selected or elected persons to represent them) were recorded in Vestry Minutes. Years ago the Vestry approved the appointment of Churchwardens and Parish Clerks and looked after Glebe Terriers - records of Church property. Thus as the Church became involved in secular matters, education, probate and social security, so the Vestry was involved with Church appointments, albeit of lay officials.

However, in urban areas Vestries developed into Borough Councils and later, District Councils, while in rural areas Parish Councils were established from 1894 to deal with secular matters. Parochial Church Councils were set up in 1921 to look after local ecclesiastical matters.

Besides the secular office of Overseer of the Poor, the Vestry appointed an Overseer of the Highway or Waywarden, a Hedgewarden, a Constable and his assistant the Pindar or Keeper of the Pound, and a host of other parish appointments, and minded the documents arising from the Inclosure and Tithe Commutation Acts of the early 19th Century. Many parish officials recorded their activities and maintained accounts which were submitted to the Vestry for approval. The Constable, for example, was responsible for listing Militiamen, keeping law and order and taking those who defaulted to magistrates at petty or quarter sessions (see below), recording these events in notebooks. Most parishes were endowed with a modest charity, some associated with schooling, set up by a local benefactor, for which accounts were kept. The parish filing system for all these documents, terriers, minutes, accounts and notebooks was a wooden chest in the church. Most of this material from the Parish Chests is now at the CRO although some, such as the Bedford Corporation (Borough) Minute Book (1647-

1664) and the Churchwardens' Accounts for Clifton (1543, 1589-1608), Northill (1561-1612), Shillington (1571-1604) and Turvey (1551-52) have been transcribed, indexed and published by BHRS in vols 26, 33 and 69, and so are available in libraries throughout the county.

A typical borough administration dealt with items such as civic jurisdiction, town properties, public health, trades, freemen, apprentices, charities, churches and military matters. Bedford was an ancient (pre-12th Century) borough; other Municipal Boroughs (Corporations) created in the county in the 19th Century were Dunstable (1864) and Luton (1876), which was a County Borough from 1964 to 1974. The extent of the Bedford Borough archives was described by Chris Pickford in the *Journal of BFHS* [34]; most Bedford Borough archives are held at Bedford Town Hall (see Chapter 7) but the CRO holds some original material {Bor.B} and microfilm copies of other Borough material. The CRO also has all the Dunstable archives {Bor.D} and some Luton {Bor.L} material while most Luton Borough (Corporation) records are at Luton Town Hall. The CRO can advise on the whereabouts of others in the county.

Manorial and Land Records

In addition to the Church and central and local government being interested in the welfare of your ancestors, and the services your ancestors could return to these systems, the lords of the manors operated in a third distinct and ancient administrative system associated with land tenure, particularly in rural areas. A manor could encompass a number of parishes or there could be several small manors in one parish; as the manorial system declined such manors disappeared or became hamlets within the parish.

Manors within a county are usefully identified under hundreds and parishes in the indexed *Victoria County History* (*VCH*) series. In towns it was possible to buy freedom from the land tenure system. Even before the Norman invasion of 1066 most land belonged to the king who let portions of it to his vassals under certain conditions, normally providing military or agricultural services. William I reinforced this system but enabled the greater and lesser barons, the lords, to let portions of their lands, their manors, to tenants under similar conditions of servitude although the lords still rendered homage to the king. The Lord of the Manor, or his representative, lived at the Manor House with his family whilst his tenants lived throughout the manor. Copyhold tenure, and gradually freehold, and finally leasehold tenure grew from the manorial system.

A series of Manorial Courts was set up to administer the procedures, collect rents and admonish those who failed to pay or broke certain terms of the tenures. The records of the Courts Baron, Leet and Customary, in Latin until 1733, are useful for family historians because copyhold tenure enabled land to be passed from generation to generation with the approval of the manorial court - and at certain court sittings the names of all the tenants are listed. Because manorial records and rolls were regarded as the lord's or his steward's personal documents, many have not been deposited in official archives, and those that are deposited are in a variety of places. However, the Manorial Documents Register of the Historical Manuscripts Commission [35] has a complete list of the locations of all known manorial documents. The CRO has a copy of the *VCH* for Bedfordshire on the open shelves in the Search Room and holds many manorial records for manors {MANOR Court & Accounts Rolls <place>}. Some manorial records, e.g., for Chalgrave, Blunham and Eggington, have been transcribed, translated, indexed and published by BHRS (vols 28 and 69).

Associated with manorial records from the 13th to the 17th Centuries are Inquisitiones Post Mortem (Questions After Death, asked by the Crown when a landowner died if the sovereign had an interest in the land) and Extenta Manerii (descriptions of the manors of the deceased). Although in Latin and kept at the PRO, these records can supply useful genealogical data as a landowner's heir and age are stated. Details of these records are indexed at the CRO under {MANOR Inquisitions PM <place>}.

From time to time, individuals and bodies (both ecclesiastical and secular authorities) who acquired the ownership of parcels of land chose to let or lease that land, or transfer it by sale or otherwise, to other individuals or bodies. Typical land records, such as maps and property records, including deeds, have been described in Chapter 2.

Another type of record associated with a change in land ownership was a Marriage Settlement, the agreement or indenture made around the time of a marriage, mainly of middle and upper classes, on the "portion" that a bride brought to the matrimonial union. The CRO has references in the main index to marriage settlements {FAMILIES/marriage settlements/<name>}.

Petty & Quarter Sessions and Assizes

Magistrates, originally as Keepers of the Peace and then Justices of the Peace, have been appointed in every shire and county for centuries. They normally met in sessions every three months, quarterly, and hence the name. The records maintained by Clerks of Peace of these Quarter Sessions are full of names, probably of your ancestors. The justices and clerks dealt with law and order, and so maintained rolls and files (with case papers), record and order books, depositions (written statements) of witnesses, recognizances (financial obligations), presentments and minutes (with verdicts and decisions) and lists of jurors and also kept lists of freeholders. However, they also supervised the administration of the Poor Laws and issued numerous licences for activities such as killing or keeping game, operating alehouses and nonconformist chapels and printing presses in return for taxes or duties paid. If anyone, perhaps also your ancestor, failed to comply with the regulations to serve or pay or obtain a licence, the magistrate gave his verdict or passed sentence.

The detection of crime, as well as failing to pay taxes and committing other indiscretions, were local matters for which the Vestry (see above) appointed a Parish Constable, in some places aided by voluntary organisations, often termed Associations for the Protection of Felons or Felons' Associations. County Police Forces were established in England and Wales from 1839. Do not forget that some offences, particularly of a moral nature, were dealt with by Church officials at sittings of Ecclesiastical Courts (see page 18). Certain elements of law and order were settled by the Manorial Courts (see above).

Serious offences were referred to judges on circuit at Assizes which were generally held twice a year. Bedfordshire was in the Norfolk Circuit until 1876 and from then until 1971 in the South Eastern Circuit. The names of individuals held in gaol, prior to appearing at Quarter Sessions or Assizes, or as a result of a sentence held in goal prior to transportation or committed to the House of Correction are on goal lists, many of which have survived. Coroners, elected by freeholders until 1888 and appointed by county councils thereafter, were responsible for investigating sudden, unnatural or suspicious deaths and deaths in prisons.

Assize records which have survived, such as Gaol Books, Precedent Books Process Books, Agenda Books, Minute Books, Indictments, Depositions, Estreats and Correspondence and County Prisons Registers, Calendars of Prisoners, Criminal Registers and Petitions from Criminals and their Families, are mostly at the PRO [36]. However, there are some assize papers (1653-88) {HSA} which include references to Bunyan in the CRO. Among the many records in the CRO for Quarter Sessions {QS} held in Bedfordshire are Jury Lists (1780-1888),

Freeholders' Books (1760-1825), Quarter Sessions Rolls and Files (1714-1980) {QSR}, Sessions Minute Books (1711-1980) {QSM}, printed Calendars of Prisoners (1800-1907), County Goal Registers of Prisoners (1799-1879) {QGV and PRIS (after 1876)} with photographs of prisoners (1859-76) and indexed 1799-1816 {QGV 10/1}, Registers of Police Service (1840-71), Deputations to Gamekeepers (1767-1916) and a large collection of Inclosure Maps and Awards (1742-1891). There is a calendar of the Sessions Rolls (1714-1832) with indexes of persons, places and subjects in the Search Room. Quarter Sessions records specifically for Bedford Borough are held at the Town Hall Muniment Room (see Chapter 7): i.e., Minutes (1771-1831 and 1846-1955), and Rolls (1750-1836).

Petty sessions in Bedfordshire were held from the 1830s at Ampthill, Bedford, Biggleswade, Leighton Buzzard, Luton, Sharnbrook (Bletsoe until 1871) and Woburn. The minutes of these sessions {PS}, and additional records for Luton, to at least the First World War, are in the CRO.

Coroners records for Bedfordshire until the 15th Century are in the PRO; some early records (1265-1413) were translated, indexed and published by BHRS (vol 41). Material from the 19th Century is in the CRO, although the records {CO} are closed for 75 years. However, reports of even recent inquests can often be found, vividly described in many cases, in local newspapers (see above). Similarly, many cases brought up at the Assizes, or Quarter or Petty Sessions were reported in newspapers, both local and national (if likely to sell additional copies); it is sometimes possible to discover information in these reports not to be found in official documents.

Military Ancestors

The regular (Standing) army has its pure origins in 1661 when the unconstitutional New Model of Oliver Cromwell was being disbanded by Charles II and the Restoration Parliament. There had always been (since 1181 at least) a territorial force; the Assize of Arms in that year required all freemen over the age of fifteen to keep weapons in their homes, initially to "abate the power of felons" and keep the peace but in reality to act as a Militia (although that term was not used until 1641) for the defence of the country. Apart from 1916-19 and 1939-60, when Britain used conscription for its military forces, the regular army has comprised volunteers who had chosen a military life-time career. A naval fleet, from which the Royal Navy developed, was constitutionally recognised well over 200 years before the army, perhaps because it posed a limited threat in a possible civil war. The Marines, established in 1690, became the Royal Marines in 1802. The Royal Air Force grew out of the Royal Flying Corps in 1918.

Colonel James Douglas's Regiment of Foot was one of twelve regiments raised in 1688, renamed the 16th Regiment of Foot in 1751 and again renamed in 1782 as the 16th (Buckinghamshire) Foot and in 1809 as the 16th (Bedfordshire) Regiment of Foot, Buckinghamshire becoming the 14th (Buckinghamshire) Regiment. From 1881 this became the 1st and 2nd Battalions of the Bedfordshire Regiment, the 3rd Battalion being the Bedford Militia and the 4th Battalion the Hertford Militia. In 1919 it became the Bedfordshire and Hertfordshire Regiment. In 1958 the Bedfordshire and Hertfordshire Regiment was amalgamated with the Essex Regiment and became the 3rd East Anglian Regiment (16th/44th Foot). This was redesignated in 1964 and again in 1968 when it became the 3rd Battalion, The Royal Anglian Regiment; it was renamed the 3rd Battalion (Bedfordshire, Hertfordshire and Essex) in 1980 and disbanded in 1992. The principal battles and campaigns in which the Bedfordshire Regiment participated are given in Chapter 7; those at which Honours on the Colours were received are identified.

In tracing the service career of a military ancestor you should refer to the records of the Army, Royal Navy, Royal Marines or Royal Air Force which are at the PRO in London (Kew). Further details on military records are given in *Tracing Your British Ancestors* [37]. Some Bedfordshire Regimental archives are held at the CRO {X 550} while the artifacts are in Luton Museum. All these addresses are in Chapter 7.

Some Bedfordshire Militia records from 1759 to 1884 were published in 1884 [38]. Muster Rolls and Books, Ballot Lists and Posse Comitatus Lists are at the CRO and at the PRO. The lieutenancy papers in the CRO contain rolls of the Bedfordshire Militia (1852-72) {LC/mil 2-3} and of the local Rifle Volunteers (later the 3rd Volunteers Battalion Bedfordshire Regiment) 1860-92 {LC/vol 3}. There is also a detailed Muster List {X 550/6/2} for the Bedford town companies of the volunteers (1864-1901).

There is a variety of sources for the First World War, including registers of absent voters and parish rolls of honour. The records for the Second World War, whilst not so comprehensive, include some Home Guard rolls {W/HGN and X 393/21}. The CRO can advise on what is available, but indexed Muster Lists from documents at the PRO and CRO for various Hundreds within Bedfordshire from 1539 to 1831 were published by BHRS (vol 71). Included in that volume are names of Bedfordshire soldiers impressed for service in Ireland (1591-1602), New Model Army deserters (1645-46), Militia Rolls and County Militia Enrolments, Ballot Lists and National Defence Lists (1803).

Heraldry

If you believe that one of your ancestors was armigerous (was granted an armorial achievement - a coat of arms - by the College of Arms), that fact will have been recorded by one of the heralds. You should appreciate that there is no such thing as a Family Coat of Arms. An individual was given a coat of arms by a herald on behalf of the monarch for services rendered to the Crown. Under specific circumstances the children of an armiger could also display the arms of their father, indicated with some mark of difference; this, and their pedigree, had to be registered with the heralds at the College. In the 16th and 17th Centuries the heralds travelled the country on their visitations, to check who was displaying which arms and to record their pedigrees from the original armiger. The pedigrees recorded were not always complete; embarrassing or inconsequential family members were conveniently forgotten and occasionally some "ancestors" were found to add prestige to a family. As a consequence Visitation Pedigrees should be verified from other sources wherever possible. The heralds visited Bedfordshire in 1566, 1582 and 1634 and again in 1669. Copies of the *Heralds' Visitations* for Bedfordshire were published by the Harleian Society in 1884 (Vol 19). F A Blaydes compiled numerous hand-written pedigrees, based on these visitations, which are now in the Society of Genealogists' Library. A series of 100 articles on the county's armigerous families, by F W Kuhlicke entitled 'A Bedfordshire Armorial' appeared in the *Bedfordshire Magazine* from 1948 to 1978. The CRO {X 171/64-68} has some magnificent heraldic illustrations.

When armigers died, their coats of arms were paraded on hatchments at their funerals. After a ceremony a funeral hatchment was sometimes hung in the parish church; in some Bedfordshire churches such hatchments are still there to this day. Bedfordshire hatchments appear in Volume 4 of Peter Summers's *Hatchments in Britain* series.

During the late 18th and throughout the 19th and 20th Centuries, numerous books have been published on coats of arms that were awarded to individuals ranging from the lower ranks of the gentry to royal dukes. Copies of many of these publications are at the CRO and libraries throughout the county.

5. Bedfordshire Parishes and Hamlets

Bedfordshire parishes and hamlets are listed in this chapter. They are arranged in alphabetical order with the date of the first entry in a parish register, if a Peculiar (Pec), the Hundred (Hd) or Borough (Bor), the Poor Law Union (Un), and thus the Registration District in which each parish originally appeared, and the CRO parish reference {P<Number>}. P- indicates that the registers have not been deposited at the CRO. Some parish registers, as indicated, are held at other records offices; their addresses are in Chapter 7. In most cases the Ecclesiastical and Civil parish are the same, but in some instances there is only an Ecclesiastical parish (†) and in others only a Civil parish (§).

The names of many hamlets were based on townships or manors as found in the Domesday Survey of 1086. Hamlets such as Church End, East End, West End have not been included here as such place names occur in many parishes.

In many cases there are gaps in the register entries. The footnotes are explained at the end of the list. A full list of the registers held in the county archives of baptisms, marriages and burials is available from the CRO.

Aley Green; a hamlet in Caddington.
Ampthill 1604; Hd Redbornestoke; Un Ampthill; P30.[M]
Arlesey 1538; Hd Clifton; Un Biggleswade; P37.[M]
Aspley Guise 1563; Hd Manshead; Un Woburn; P122.[M][a][b]
§Aspley Heath created 1883/5; Hds Manshead & Newport Pagnell; Un Woburn.[b][c]
Astwick 1564; Hd Biggleswade; Un Biggleswade; P98.
Barford, Great 1559; Hd Barford; Un Bedford; P23.[M]
Barford, Little 1661; Hd Biggleswade; Un St Neots; P56.[M][d]
Barton in the Clay 1558; Hd Flitt; Un Luton; P21.[M][e]
Barworth; a hamlet in Studham.
Battlesden 1677; Hd Manshead; Un Woburn; P102.[M][b]
†Bedford, All Saints 1895; Bor Bedford; Un Bedford; P141.
†Bedford, Christ Church 1920; Bor Bedford; Un Bedford; P121.
†Bedford, Holy Trinity 1841; Bor Bedford; Un Bedford; P133.
†Bedford, St Andrew 1915; Bor Bedford; Un Bedford; P131.
Bedford, St Cuthbert 1607; Bor Bedford; Un Bedford; P120.[M]
Bedford, St John 1669; Bor Bedford; Un Bedford; P88.[M]
†Bedford, St Leonard 1889; Bor Bedford; Un Bedford; P134.
†Bedford, St Mark 1983; Bor Bedford; Reg Dist Bedford; P146.
†Bedford, St Martin 1896; Bor Bedford; Un Bedford; P147.
Bedford, St Mary 1539; Bor Bedford; Un Bedford; P81.[B][M]
†Bedford, St Michael 1934; Bor Bedford; Reg Dist Bedford; P156.
Bedford, St Paul 1565; Bor Bedford; Un Bedford; P1.[M]
Bedford, St Peter 1572; Bor Bedford; Un Bedford; P100.[B]

Beeston; a hamlet in Sandy/Northill.

Biddenham 1663; Hd Willey; Un Bedford; P74.[f]

Bidwell; a hamlet in Houghton Regis.

Biggleswade 1697; (Pec); Hd Biggleswade; Un Biggleswade; P14.[M]

Billington 1653; civ par created 1866; (Pec); Hd Manshead; Un Leighton Buzzard; P111.

Biscot (Bishopcote); see Limbury-cum-Biscot.

Bletsoe 1582; Hd Willey; Un Bedford; P36.

Blunham 1571; Hd Wixamtree; Un Biggleswade; P76.[M]

Bolnhurst 1685; Hd Stodden; Un Bedford; P46.

§Bolnhurst & Keysoe created 1933/4 from Bolnhurst and Keysoe.

§Brogborough created 1989 from Husborne Crawley & Ridgmont.

Bromham 1570; Hd Willey; Un Bedford; P67.[M]

Broom; a hamlet in Southill.

Budna; a hamlet in Northill.

Bushmead; a hamlet in Eaton Socon.

Caddington 1558; Hds Dacorum & Flitt; Un Luton; P35.[M][g][h]

§Caddington & Slip End created 1933 when part of ecc par trans to Luton.

Cainhoe; a hamlet in Clophill.

†Caldecote 1928; a former hamlet in Northill; P142.

Campton 1568; Hd Clifton; Un Biggleswade; P18.[M]

§Campton & Chicksands created 1985 from Campton and Chicksands.

Cardington 1572; Hd Wixamtree; Un Bedford; P38.[M][d]

Carlton 1554; Hd Willey; Un Bedford; P92.[i]

§Carlton & Chellington; created 1934; but see footnote [i].

Chalgrave 1539; Hd Manshead; Un Woburn; P114.[M][g][j][k]

Chalton; a hamlet in Toddington.

Channel's End; a hamlet in Colmworth.

Charlton; a hamlet in Moggerhanger.

Chaul End; a hamlet in Caddington.

Chawston; a hamlet in Roxton.

Chellington 1567; Hd Willey; Un Bedford; P145.[i]

§Chicksands; ex par; see Campton. created 1858 in Hd Clifton; Un Biggleswade.

Clapham 1696; Hd Stodden; Un Bedford; P117.[f]

Clifton 1538; Hd Clifton; Un Biggleswade; P7.[M]

Clipston; a hamlet in Eggington.

Clophill 1567; Hd Flitt; Un Ampthill; P45.[M]

Cockayne Hatley 1701; Hd Biggleswade; Un Biggleswade; P104.[M]

Colesden; a hamlet in Roxton.

Colmworth 1735; Hd Barford; Un Bedford; P47.[M]

§Colworth; formerly ex-parochial, created 1858 in Hd Wixamtree; Un Bedford; amalgamated with
    Sharnbrook in 1895.

Cople 1563; Hd Wixamtree; Un Bedford; P4.[M]

Cotton End; a hamlet in Cardington.

Covington; a hamlet in Pertenhall.

Cranfield 1600; Hd Redbornestoke; Un Ampthill; P62.

Dean, Nether 1566; Hd Stodden; Un St Neots; P109.[d]

§Dean & Shelton created 1934 from Dean and Shelton.

Denel End; a hamlet in Flitwick.

Dilwick; a hamlet in Stagsden.

Duloe; a hamlet in Eaton Socon.

†Dunstable, St Augustine 1959; Reg Dist Dunstable; P140.

†Dunstable, St Fremund 1968; Reg Dist Dunstable; P154.

Dunstable, St Peter 1558; Hd Manshead; Un Luton; P72.[B][M][g]

Dunton 1553; Hd Biggleswade; Un Biggleswade; P51.[M]

§Eastcotts; a hamlet in Cardington; created a Civil parish 1866.[f]

East Hyde; see Hyde, East.

Eaton Bray 1559; Hd Manshead; Un Leighton Buzzard; P63.[M][g][l]

Eaton Ford; a hamlet in Eaton Socon.

Eaton Socon 1566; Hd Barford; Un St Neots; P5.[d][m]

Edlesborough 1567; in Bkm; registers at Bkm CRO (see Chapter 7).

Edworth 1552; Hd Biggleswade; Un Biggleswade; P110.

Eggington 1813; (Pec); formerly in Leighton Buzzard; Hd Manshead; Un Leighton Buzzard; P116.

Elstow 1641; Hd Redbornestoke; Un Bedford; P128.[M][f]

Eversholt 1628; Hd Manshead; Un Woburn; P42.[M][b]

Everton 1650; (partly in Hun, some trans in 1844) Hd Biggleswade; Un Biggleswade; P53.[M][n]

Eyeworth 1538; Hd Biggleswade; Un Biggleswade; P19.[M]

Fancott; a hamlet in Toddington.

Farndish 1587; Hds Willey & Higham Ferrers; Un Wellingborough; P126.[B][o]

Felmersham 1660; Hd Willey; Un Bedford; P93.

Fenlake; a hamlet in Cardington.

Flitton 1518; Hd Flitt; Un Ampthill; P12.[M]

§Flitton & Greenfield created 1932 from Flitton and Pulloxhill.

Flitwick 1661; Hd Redbornestoke; Un Ampthill; P59.[B]

Girtford; a hamlet in Sandy.

Gladley; a hamlet in Heath and Reach.

Goldington 1559; Hd Barford; Un Bedford; P78.[p]

Gravenhurst, Lower 1705; Hd Flitt; Un Ampthill; P144.[M][q]

Gravenhurst, Upper 1567; Hd Flitt; Un Ampthill; P17.[M][q]

Great Barford; see Barford, Great.

Greenfield; a hamlet in Flitton and Pulloxhill.

Harlington 1653; Hd Manshead; Un Woburn; P75.[M][b]

Harrold 1598; Hd Willey; Un Bedford; P33.

Harrowden; a hamlet in Cardington.

Hassells; a hamlet in Sandy/Clifton/Stotfold.

Hatch; a hamlet in Northill.

Hatley; a former name of Cockayne Hatley.

Hawnes; an alternative spelling of Haynes.

Haynes 1596; Hd Flitt; Un Ampthill; P6.[M]

Heath and Reach 1813 (formerly a chapelry of Leighton Buzzard); (Pec); Hd Manshead; Un Leighton Buzzard; P84.[r]

Henlow 1558; Hd Clifton; Un Biggleswade; P39.[M]

Herne; a hamlet in Toddington/Chalgrave.

Hexton 1538; in Hrt; regs at Hrt CRO (see Chapter 7).

Higham Gobion 1654; Hd Flitt; Un Ampthill; P125.[M]

Hinwick; a hamlet in Podington.

Hockliffe 1696; Hd Manshead; Un Woburn; P103.[M][g]

Holcot; an alternative spelling of Hulcote.
Holme; a hamlet in Biggleswade.
Holwell 1560; Hd Clifton; Un Hitchin; trans to Hrt in 1897.[M]
Honeydon; a hamlet in Eaton Socon.
Houghton Conquest 1595; Hd Redbornestoke; Un Ampthill; P11.[M]
Houghton Regis 1538; Hd Manshead; Un Luton; P101.[M][g][s]
Hulcote 1658; Hd Manshead; Un Woburn; P113.[b][t]
§Hulcote & Salford created 1933 from Hulcote and Salford.
Humbershoe; a hamlet in Studham, trans to Hrt in 1888.
Husborne Crawley 1558; Hd Manshead; Un Ampthill; P49.[M]
§Hyde created 1895; formerly a hamlet of Luton.
Hyde, East 1841; Hd Flitt; Un Luton; P-.
Ickleford 1749; partly in Hrt until trans in 1832/44.
Ickwell; a hamlet in Northill.
Kempston, All Saints 1570; Hd Redbornestoke; Un Bedford; P60.
§Kempston Rural created 1895 from outlying parts of Kempston which did not join Bedford.
Kempston, St John 1868; Hd Redbornestoke; Un Bedford; in P139.
Kempston, St Stephen 1887; Hd Redbornestoke; Un Bedford; in P139.
Kempston, Transfiguration 1940; Reg Dist Bedford; P139.
Kensworth 1615; Hd Dacorum; Un Luton; trans from Hrt in 1897; P34.[g]
Keysoe 1735; Hd Stodden; Un Bedford; P48.
Kinwick; a hamlet in Sandy.
Knotting 1592; Hd Stodden; Un Bedford; P107.
§Knotting & Souldrop created 1933/4.
Langford 1717; Hd Biggleswade; Un Biggleswade; P99.
Leagrave; formerly a hamlet in Limbury; see Luton, St Luke.[u]
Leighton Buzzard, All Saints 1562; (Pec); Hd Manshead; Un Leighton Buzzard; P91.[M]
†Leighton Buzzard, St Andrew 1868; Hd Manshead; Un Leighton Buzzard; in P91.
§Leighton-Linslade created 1965 from Leighton Buzzard and Linslade, Bkm.
Lewsey; a hamlet in Luton.
Lidlington 1564; Hd Redbornestoke; Un Ampthill; P2.
Limbury-cum-Biscot 1866; formerly a hamlet in Luton; P-.[u]
Little Barford; see Barford, Little.
Little Staughton; see Staughton, Little.
Lower Gravenhurst; see Gravenhurst, Lower.
†Luton, All Saints 1922; Hd Flitt; Un Luton; P137.
†Luton, Christ Church 1860; Hd Flitt; Un Luton; P135.
†Luton, Holy Cross (Marsh Farm) 1968; Reg Dist Luton; P-.
†Luton, St Andrew 1887; Hd Flitt; Un Luton; P150.
†Luton, St Anne 1938; Reg Dist Luton; P151.
†Luton, St Augustine 1966; created from Limbury-cum-Biscot in 1971; P149.
†Luton, St Christopher (Round Green) 1939; Reg Dist Luton; P-.
†Luton, St Francis 1960; Reg Dist Luton; P153.
†Luton, St Hugh (Cockernhoe) 1955; Reg Dist Luton; in P153.
†Luton, St Hugh (Lewsey) 1961; Reg Dist Luton; P152.
†Luton, St John the Baptist (Farley Hill) 1966; Reg Dist Luton; P-.
†Luton, St Luke (Leagrave) 1936; Reg Dist Luton; P-.
Luton, St Mary 1603; Hd Flitt; Un Luton; P85.[B][M]

†Luton, St Matthew (High Town) 1877; Hd Flitt; Un Luton; P132.
†Luton, St Paul (New Town) 1895; Hd Flitt; Un Luton; P155.
†Luton, St Peter 1913; Hd Flitt; Un Luton; P136.
†Luton, St Saviour 1884; Hd Flitt; Un Luton; P138.
Markyate 1855; regsiters at Hrt CRO (see Chapter 7).
§Markyate Street; trans to Hrt 1904.
Marston Moretaine 1653; Hd Redbornestoke; Un Ampthill; P41.
Maulden 1558; Hd Redbornestoke; Un Ampthill; P31.[M]
Melchbourne 1706; Hd Stodden; Un Bedford; P73.
§Melchbourne & Yelden created 1933/4 from Melchbourne and Y(i)elden.
Meppershall 1652; partly in Hrt until trans in 1832-44; Hd Clifton; Un Biggleswade; P29.
Millbrook 1558; Hd Redbornestoke; Un Woburn; P95.[b]
Millow; a hamlet in Dunton.
Milton Bryan 1559; Hd Manshead; Un Woburn; P15.[M][b]
Milton Ernest 1538; Hd Stodden; Un Bedford; P80.
Moddry; a hamlet in Clophill.
Moggerhanger 1860 (formerly a hamlet in Blunham); civ par created 1866; P143.
Mosbury; a hamlet in Everton.
Newton; a hamlet in Dunton.
Northill 1562; Hd Wixamtree; Un Biggleswade; P10.[M][v]
Notley; a hamlet in Sundon.
Oakley 1560; Hd Stodden; Un Bedford; P40.
Odell 1604; Hd Willey; Un Bedford; P115.
Old Warden; see Warden, Old.
Pavenham 1561; Hd Willey; Un Bedford; P68.
Pegsdon; a hamlet in Shillington.
Pertenhall 1582: Hd Stodden; Un St Neots; P65.[d]
Pict's Hill; a hamlet in Stevington.
Podington 1662; Hd Willey; Un Wellingborough; P127.[B][o]
Polehanger; a hamlet in Meppershall.
Potsgrove 1663; Hd Manshead; Un Woburn; P124.[M][b]
Potton 1614; Hd Biggleswade; Un Biggleswade; P64.[M]
Priestly; a hamlet in Flitwick.
Puddington; an alternative name for Podington.
Puddlehill; a hamlet in Houghton Regis.
Pulloxhill 1553; Hd Flitt; Un Ampthill; P13.[M]
Putnoe; a hamlet in Goldington.
Radwell; a hamlet in Felmersham; (do not confuse with Hrt hamlet of Radwell adjacent to Stotfold).
Ramridge End; a hamlet in Stopsley.
Ravensden 1558; Hd Barford; Un Bedford; P89.
Renhold 1654; Hd Barford; Un Bedford; P32.
Ridgmont 1539; Hd Redbornestoke; Un Woburn; P43.[b]
Riseley 1626; Hd Stodden; Un Bedford; P50.
Risinghoe; a hamlet in Goldington.
Rowney: a part of Southill.
Roxton 1684; Hd Barford; Un Bedford; P28.[M]
Salford 1559; Hd Manshead. Un Woburn; P77.[b][t]
Salph End; a hamlet in Renhold.

Sandy 1538; Hds Biggleswade & Wixamtree; Un Biggleswade; P9.[M]
Seddington; a hamlet in Sandy.
Segenhoe; a hamlet in Ridgmont.
Segresdon; a hamlet in Pertenhall.
Sewell; a hamlet in Houghton Regis.
Sharnbrook 1595; Hd Willey; Un Bedford; P112.
Sharpenhoe; a hamlet in Streatley.
Shefford 1873 (early entries in Campton); civ par created 1866; Hd Clifton; Un Biggleswade; P70.
§Shefford Hardwicke; ex parochial, created a civil parish 1903.
Shelton 1706; Hd Stodden; Un St Neots; P94.[d]
Shelton; a hamlet in Marston Moretaine.
Shillington 1543; Hds Odsey (Hrt), Clifton & Flitt; Un Ampthill; P44.[M][w]
Silsoe 1846 (previously a hamlet of Flitton); Hd Flitt; Un Ampthill; P54.
Slip End; see Woodside.
Souldrop 1670; Hd Willey; Un Bedford; P108.
Southill 1538; Hd Wixamtree; Un Biggleswade; P69.[M]
South Mills. A hamlet in Blunham.
Stagsden 1670; Hd Willey; Un Bedford; P79.[M]
Stanbridge 1560; (Pec); Hd Manshead; Un Leighton Buzzard; P57.
Stanford; a hamlet in Southill.
Staploe created 1965; formerly a hamlet in Eaton Socon.
Staughton, Little 1598; Hd Stodden; Un St Neots; P66.[d]
Steppingley 1558; Hd Redbornestoke; Un Ampthill; P82.
Stevington 1654; Hd Willey; Un Bedford; P71.[M]
§Stewartby created 1937 out of Wootton and Kempston Rural.
Stondon, Upper 1683; Hd Clifton; Un Biggleswade; P55.
Stopsley 1863; a former hamlet of Luton; Hd Flitt; Un Luton; P-.[x]
Stotfold 1559; Hd Clifton; Un Biggleswade; P83.[M]
Stratford; a hamlet in Sandy.
Stratton; a hamlet in Biggleswade.
Streatley 1693; Hd Flitt; Un Luton; P25.[M][y]
Studham 1570; trans from Hun 1897; Hds Dacorum & Manshead; Un Luton; P86.[B][M][g]
Sudbury; a hamlet in Eaton Socon.
Sundon 1592; Hd Flitt; Un Luton; P24.[M][y]
Sutton 1538; Hd Biggleswade; Un Biggleswade; P123.[M]
Swanton; a hamlet in Harrold.
Swineshead 1549; tran from Hun 1897; Hd Leightonstone; Un St Neots; P96.[d]
Tebworth; a hamlet in Chalgrave.
Temple Hills; a hamlet in Sharnbrook.
Tempsford 1604; Hd Biggleswade; Un Biggleswade; P20.[M]
Tetworth; a hamlet in Everton; Hd Toseland; Un St Neots.
Thorn; a hamlet in Houghton Regis.
Thorncote; a hamlet in Northill.
Thurleigh 1562; Hd Willey; Un Bedford; P97.
Tilbrook 1573; trans to Hun 1896; Hd Stodden; Un St Neots. Registers at Hun RO.[z]
Tilsworth 1649; Hd Manshead; Un Woburn; P130.[M][j]
Tingrith 1572; Hd Manshead; Un Woburn; P90.[M][b]
Toddington 1558; Hd Manshead; Un Woburn; P8.[M][b][g]

Totternhoe 1559; Hd Manshead; Un Luton; P58.[M][g]
Turvey 1629; Hd Willey; Un Bedford; P27.[M]
Upbury; a hamlet in Pulloxhill.
Upper Gravenhurst; see Gravenhurst, Upper.
Upper Stondon; see Stondon, Upper.
Wadlowes; a hamlet in Toddington.
Warden, Old 1576; Hd Wixamtree; Un Biggleswade; P105.[M]
Westcotts; a hamlet in Wils(hamps)tead.
Westoning 1560; Hd Manshead; Un Ampthill; P16.[M]
Whipsnade 1682; Hds Manshead & Dacorum; Un Luton; part in Hrt until 1897; P87.[M][g]
Wilden 1545; Hd Barford; Un Bedford; P106.[M]
Willington 1676; Hd Wixamtree; Un Bedford; P26.[M]
Wils(hamps)tead 1593; Hd Redbornestoke; Un Bedford; P22.[M]
Wingfield; a hamlet in Chalgrave.
Woburn 1558; Hd Manshead; Un Woburn; P118.[M][b] (do not confuse with Wooburn, Bkm).
†Woburn Sands 1868; cr 1867 from Aspley Guise & Wavendon, Bkm. Hd Manshead; Un Woburn;
        P129 [b].
Woodcroft; a hamlet in Luton.
Woodside with Slip End 1879 (formerly in Caddington) Hds Dacorum & Flitt; Un Luton; P148.
Wootton 1562; Hd Redbornestoke; Un Bedford; P3.
Wrestlingworth 1578; Hd Biggleswade; Un Biggleswade; P52.[M]
§Wrestlingworth & Cockayne Hatley created 1933/4 from Wrestlingworth and Cockayne Hatley.
Wyboston; a hamlet in Eaton Socon.
Wymington 1662; Hd Willey; Un Wellingborough; P61.[d]
Y(i)elden 1653; Hd Stodden; Un Bedford; P119.

[B] marriages for some years are indexed in P Boyd's Miscellaneous Series; see page 19 above.
[M] some monumental inscriptions were transcribed by A Weight Matthews; see page 23 above.

[a] a small portion of Aspley Guise was in Buckinghamshire.
[b] transferred to Ampthill Union on 26 September 1899.
[c] Aspley Heath was created from part of Aspley Guise (1883) and Wavendon, Bkm (1885).
[d] transferred to Bedford Registration District on 1 October 1935.
[e] Barton in the Clay was renamed Barton-le-Clay in 1956.
[f] part transferred for civil purposes to Bedford in 1933.
[g] transferred to Dunstable Registration District on 1 April 1964.
[h] Caddington was partly in Hertfordshire until 1894/7; part trans to Luton in 1928 & 1933 when part
        also trans to Dunstable.
[i] Carlton and Chellington were a consolidated eccl parish before 1801 and after 1972.
[j] transferred to Leighton Buzzard Union on 26 September 1899.
[k] part of Chalgrave was transferred for civil purposes to Hockliffe in 1929.
[l] Eaton Bray was transferred from Luton Union in 1846.
[m] part transferred to Hun on 1 April 1965 which became Cam in 1974; the remaining part, for civil
        purposes only, was renamed Staploe.
[n] Everton was historically (and still is) in Ely Diocese, whereas the remainder of Bdf is now in St
        Albans Diocese; records at County Record Office, Grammar School Walk, Huntingdon,
        PE18 6LF. Tel: 01480-425842.

[o] Farndish, Podington and Wymington were transferred from Wellingborough Registration District to Bedford Reg Dist on 1 July 1936. Podington & Farndish were combined in 1970.

[p] Goldington was transferred in total for civil purposes to Bedford in 1933.

[q] Lower Gravenhurst and Upper Gravenhurst were amalgamated in 1888 but abolished in 1972 to create Upper & Lower Gravenhurst.

[r] Heath & Reach civ par created 1866; part was transferred for civil purposes to Leighton Buzzard in 1933.

[s] part of Houghton Regis was transferred for civil purposes to Dunstable in 1907 and part to Luton in 1939.

[t] Hulcote and Salford became a combined parish in 1750 but maintained separate registers.

[u] Leagrave (Limbury) created a civil parish in 1895; transferred in total to Luton in 1928; became the ecc parish of Luton St Luke in 1936.

[v] part of Northill was transferred for civil purposes to Sandy in 1933.

[w] part of Shillington was transferred for civil purposes to Hrt in 1897; part exchanged for part of Offley, Hrt in 1907.

[x] Stopsley was created a civil parish in 1895 but transferred to Luton in 1928 and 1933.

[y] part transferred for civil purposes to Luton in 1964.

[z] some earlier Tilbrook BTs from 1604 and other records are at Hrt RO (for address see Chapter 7), the central Diocesan Record Office for St Albans Diocese. The Bedford Archdeaconry parish records, belonging to the St Albans Diocese, are held by Bedford CRO.

As some of the above comments regarding boundary changes are rather complicated, you may like to look at the map on page 52 and read the text on page 4 again!

6. Parishes within Hundreds

This chapter lists Civil and Ecclesiastical Parishes and Hamlets arranged alphabetically within Hundreds.

Hundred of Barford: Colmworth, Eaton Socon, Goldington, Great Barford, Ravensden, Renhold, Roxton, Wilden.

Hundred of Biggleswade: Astwick, Beeston, Biggleswade, Chicksands, Cockayne Hatley, Dunton, Edworth, Everton, Eyworth, Girtford, Holme, Langford, Little Barford, Potton, Sandy, Shefford Hardwick, Stratton, Sutton, Tempsford, Wrestlingworth.

Hundred of Clifton: Arlesey, Campton, Clifton, Henlow, Holwell, Meppershall, Shefford, Shillington (part), Stotfold, Upper Stondon.

Hundred of Flitt: Barton-le-Cley, Biscot, Caddington, Clophill, Flitton, Haynes, Higham Gobion, Hyde (East & West), Leagrave, Limbury, Lower Gravenhurst, Luton, Pulloxhill, Sharpenhoe, Shillington (part), Silsoe, Stopsley, Streatley, Sundon, Upper Gravenhurst.

Hundred of Manshead: Aspley Guise, Battlesden, Billington, Chalgrave, Dunstable, Eaton Bray, Eggington, Eversholt, Harlington, Heath and Reach, Hockliffe, Hulcote, Houghton Regis, Humbershoe (Hrt), Husborne Crawley, Leighton Buzzard, Milton Bryan, Potsgrove, Salford, Stanbridge, Studham, Tebworth, Tilsworth, Tingrith, Toddington, Totternhoe, Westoning, Whipsnade, Wingfield, Woburn.

Hundred of Redbornestoke: Ampthill, Cranfield, Elstow, Flitwick, Houghton Conquest, Kempston, Lidlington, Marston Mortaine, Maulden, Millbrook, Ridgmont, Steppingley, Wilstead, Wootton.

Hundred of Stodden: Bolnhurst, Clapham, Dean, Keysoe, Knotting, Little Staughton, Melchbourne, Milton Ernest, Oakley, Pertenhall, Riseley, Shelton, Tilbrook, Yelden.

Hundred of Willey: Biddenham, Bletsoe, Bromham, Carlton, Chellington, Farndish, Felmersham, Harrold, Odell, Pavenham, Poddington, Sharnbrook, Souldrop, Stagsden, Stevington, Thurleigh, Turvey, Wymington.

Hundred of Wixamtree: Blunham, Cardington, Chalton, Cople, Eastcotts, Moggerhanger, Northill, Rowney, Southill, Old Warden, Willington.

Half-Hundred, Liberty or **Borough of Bedford**: St Cuthbert, St John, St Mary, St Peter, St Paul.

BEDFORDSHIRE
The HISTORIC PARISHES (c1880)

▬▬▬▬▬	Modern County Boundary
───────	Historic Parish Boundary
Linslade (Bucks)	Whole or parts of Parishes transferred to Bedfordshire since c1880
●●●●●●	Peculiar Jurisdictions

Shelton
Dean
Tilbrook
Yielden
Melchbourne
Swineshead (Hunts)
Pertenhall
Little Staughton
Wymington
Farndish
Podington
Knotting
Riseley
Keysoe
Souldrop
Odell
Sharnbrook
Bletsoe
Thurleigh
Bolnhurst
Colmworth
Eaton Socon
Harrold
Felmersham
Milton Ernest
Ravensden
Wilden
Roxton
Little Barford
Chellington
Pavenham
Carlton
Oakley
Clapham
Renhold
Great Barford
Blunham
Tempsford
Everton (Ietworth (Hunts))
Everton
Turvey
Steving-ton
Bromham
Goldington
Willington
Mogerhanger
SANDY
Potton
Cockayne Hatley
Stagsden
Bidden-ham
BEDFORD
Kempston
Elstow
Eastcotts
Cople
Cardington
Northill
Sutton
Wrestling-worth
Eyeworth
Wootton
Marston Moretaine
Houghton Conquest
Wilshamstead
Old Warden
BIGGLESWADE
Dunton
Cranfield
Salford
Hulcote
Lidlington
Millbrook
AMPTHILL
Haynes
Chicksands Priory
Southill
Langford
Edworth
Ridgmont
Holcote Crawley
Steppingley
Maulden
Clophill
Compton
Clifton
Henlow
Astwick
Aspley Guise
Wavendon (Bucks)
Woburn
Eversholt
Tingrith
Flitwick
Flitton
Pulloxhill
Silsoe
Meppershall
Gravenhurst
Upper Stondon
Arlesey
Stotfold
Shillington
Potsgrove
Milton Bryan
Westoning
Harlington
Streatley
Barton in the Clay
Higham Gobion
Heath & Reach
Battlesden
TODDINGTON
Sundon
Linslade (Bucks)
LEIGHTON BUZZARD
Hockliffe
Tilsworth
Chalgrave
Eggington
Stanbridge
Billington
Houghton Regis
LUTON
Totternhoe
Eaton Bray
Dunstable
Caddington (Beds)
Caddington (Herts)
Kensworth (Herts)
Whipsnade
Studham (Beds)
Studham (Herts)

1. Colworth
2. Shefford Hardwick
3. Shefford
4. Holwell
5. Higham Gobion
6. Harlington
7. Westoning
8. Houghton Regis
9. Studham

7 Useful Addresses etc.

County Record Office,
County Hall,
Cauldwell Street,
Bedford, MK42 9AP.
Tel: 01234-228833 or 228777.

Muniments Room,
Town Hall,
Bedford, MK40 1SJ.
Tel: 01234-267422.
[Appointment necessary]

Buckinghamshire Record Office,
County Hall,
Aylesbury, HP20 1UA.
Tel: 01296-382587.

Hertfordshire Record Office,
County Hall,
Hertford, SG13 8DE.
Tel: 01992-555105.

Cambridgeshire Record Office,
Shire Hall, Castle Hill,
Cambridge, CB3 0AP.
Tel: 01223-317281.

Northamptonshire Record Office,
Wootton Hall Park,
Northampton, NN4 8BQ.
Tel: 01604-762129.

Cambridgeshire Record Office,
Grammar School Walk,
Huntingdon, PE18 6LF.
Tel: 01480-425842.

Public Record Office,
Ruskin Avenue, Kew,
Surrey, TW9 4DU.
Tel: 0181-876-3444.

Bedfordshire Hist. Record Society,
c/o County Record Office.

Family History Societies.
See page 3.

Libraries and Family History Centres in and around Bedfordshire:

Bedford Central Library,
Local Studies Library,
Harpur Street,
Bedford, MK40 1PG.
Tel: 01234-350931.

Dunstable Library,
Vernon Place,
Dunstable, LU5 4HA.
Tel: 01582-608441.

Biggleswade Library,
Chestnut Avenue,
Biggleswade, SG18 0LL.
Tel: 01767-312324.

Flitwick Library,
Coniston Road,
Flitwick, MK45 1QJ.
Tel: 01525-715268.

Hitchin Library,
Paynes Park,
Hitchin, SG5 1EW.
Tel: 01462-450133.

Kempston Library,
Halsey Road,
Kempston, MK42 8AU.
Tel: 01234-853092.

Leighton Buzzard Library,
Lake Street,
Leighton Buzzard, LU7 8RX.
Tel: 01525-371788.

Luton Central Library,
St George's Square,
Luton, LU1 2NG.
Tel: 01582-30161.

Potton Library,
Clock House,
Potton, SG19 2NP.
Tel: 01767-260740.

Sandy Library,
Market Square,
Sandy, SG19 1EH.
Tel: 01767-80384.

Toddington Library,
9 Market Square,
Toddington, LU5 6BP.
Tel: 01525-3626.

✧✧✧

LDS Family History Centre,
Cutenhoe/London Road,
Luton, LU1 3ND.
Tel: 01582-482234.

LDS Family History Centre,
137 Harlestone Road,
Northampton, NN5 6AA.
Tel: 01604-587630

Museums in Bedfordshire:

Bedford Museum,
Castle Lane,
Bedford, MK40 3XD.
Tel: 01234-353323.

Bunyan Meeting Library & Museum,
Mill Street,
Bedford, MK40 3EU.
Tel: 01234-213722/212485.

Cecil Higgins Art Gallery & Museum,
Castle Close,
Bedford, MK40 3RP.
Tel: 01234-211222.

Bromham Water Mill,
Bridge End,
Bromham, MK43 8QS.
Tel: 01234-824330/228671.

Elstow Moot Hall,
Church End,
Elstow, MK42 9XT.
Tel: 01234-266889/228671.

Harlington Heritage Trust,
2 Shepherds Close,
Harlington, LU5 6LZ.
Tel: 01525-874683.

Leighton Buzzard Narrow Gauge Railway,
Page's Park Station, Billington Road,
Leighton Buzzard, LU7 8TN.
Tel: 01525-373888.

Luton Hoo Wernher Collection,
Wheathampstead Road,
Luton, LU1 3TQ.
Tel: 01582-22955.

Luton Museum & Art Gallery,
Wardown Park,
Luton, LU2 7HA.
Tel: 01582-746722.

Shuttleworth (aeroplane) Collection,
Old Warden Aerodrome,
Biggleswade, SG 18 9ER.
Tel: 01767-627288.

Stevington Postmill,
c/o Royal George Hotel,
Silver St, Stevington, MK43 7QN.
Tel: 01234-822184.

Stockwood Craft Museum,
Stockwood Park, Farley Hill,
Luton, LU1 4BH.
Tel: 01582-38714.

Stondon Museum,
Stampit House,
Bedford Road, Stondon, SG16 6EB.
Tel: 01582-750469 or 01933-76866.

Woburn Abbey,
Woburn,
MK17 9QN.
Tel: 01525-290666.

Woburn Heritage Centre,
St Mary's Church,
Bedford Street, Woburn, MK17 9QL.
Tel: 01525-290225.

Wrest Park House & Gardens,
Silsoe,
MK45 4HR.
Tel: 01525-860152.

Other Local History and Genealogical Contacts:

Bedfordshire Leisure Services,
County Hall,
Bedford, MK42 9AP.
Tel: 01234-228671.

Ampthill Tourist Information Centre,
12 Dunstable Street,
Ampthill, MK45 2JT.
Tel: 01525-402051, 01767-313137.

Bedford Tourist Office,
10 St Paul's Square,
Bedford, MK40 1SL.
Tel: 01234-215226.

Dunstable Tourist Office,
Vernon Place,
Dunstable, LU5 4EX.
Tel: 01582-471012.

Luton Tourist Office,
66-67 Bute Street,
Luton, LU1 2EY.
Tel: 01582-401579.

Sandy Tourist Office,
Girtford Bridge, London Road,
Sandy, SG19 1NA.
Tel: 01767-682728.

Society of Genealogists,
14 Charterhouse Buildings,
Goswell Road,
London, EC1M 7BA.
Tel: 0171-251-8799.

Family Tree Magazine,
61 Great Whyte,
Ramsay, Huntingdon,
PE17 1HL.
Tel: 01487-814050.

Civil (Superintendent) Registrars in Bedfordshire:

Bedford: Pilgrim House, 20 Brickhill Drive, Bedford, MK41 7PZ. Tel: 01234-354554.

Biggleswade: 142 London Road, Biggleswade, SG18 8EL. Tel: 01767-312511.

Ampthill: Court House, Woburn Street, Ampthill, MK45 2HX. Tel: 01525-403430.

Dunstable: 76 High Street North, Dunstable, LU6 1NF. Tel: 01582-660191.

Leighton Buzzard: Bossard Ho., West St, L'ton Buzzard, LU7 7DA. Tel: 01525-851486.

Luton: Register Office, 6 George Street West, Luton, LU1 2BJ. Tel: 01582-22603.

The 16th (Bedfordshire) Regiment of Foot

Principal campaigns and battles in which the Regiment was engaged from 1689 to 1900. See also Chapter 4.

1689-97	Flanders	1709	Tournay
1689	Walcourt	1709	*Malplaquet
1692	Steenkirk	1741	Carthagena
1693	Neer Landen	1742	Cuba
1695	Namur	1778	Baton Rouge
1702-12	Germany	1779-81	America
1702	Liege	1781	Pensacola
1704	Schellenberg	1793-94	San Domingo
1704	*Blenheim	1795	Jamaica
1706	*Ramilies	1804	*Surinam
1708	*Oudenarde	1895	*Chitral
1708	Lisle	1900	South Africa

* Honours on the Colours received.

Notes and References

1 Joyce Godber. *History of Bedfordshire 1066-1888*. 1969.
2 L R Conisbee. *Bedfordshire Bibliography*. 1962. Supplements in 1967, 1971 and to 1975 (published in 1978).
3 Bedfordshire Historical Record Society, Vol 72 pp 3-23. 1993.
4 *Pre-1841 Censuses & Population Listings in the British Isles*. Colin R Chapman. Lochin. 1994.
5 CRO *Newsletters* 3/8/87, 4/12/87, 5/3/88, 6/6/88, 9/3/89, 10/6/89, 11/9/89, 12/12/89.
6 reprinted privately in 1994.
7 CRO/BFHS. *Bedfordshire Parish Poor Law Papers 1622-1834*. Occasional Papers 2. 1991.
8 BFHS. *An Alphabetical List of Bedfordshire Strays*. Occasional Paper 1. 1990.
9 Dean, Eaton Socon, Little Barford, Pertenhall, Shelton, Little Staughton and Swineshead. Tilbrook had already been transferred (in 1986).
10 Farndish, Podington and Wymington.
11 The parishes of Caddington with Slip End, Chalgrave, Dunstable, Eaton Bray, Houghton Regis, Kensworth, Studham, Toddington, Totternhoe and Whipsnade.
12 Colin R Chapman. *Tracing Your British Ancestors*. Lochin Publishing. 1996.
13 Colin R Chapman. *Ecclesiastical Courts, Officials & Records: Sin, Sex & Probate*. Lochin. 1997.
14 Lincoln Diocesan Archives, Lincolnshire Archives, St Rumbold Street, Lincoln, LN2 5AB.
15 Ely Diocesan Records, University Library, West Road, Cambridge, CB2 9DR.
16 St Albans Diocesan Record Office, Hertfordshire Rec. Office, County Hall, Hertford, SG13 8DE.
17 These parishes are identified by B in the list in Chapter 5.
18 To access this, contact The Secretary, BFHS, PO Box 214, Bedford, MK42 9RX.
19 Colin R Chapman. *Pre-1841 Censuses & Population Listings in the British Isles*. Lochin. 1994.
20 Patricia L Bell. *Bedford's Second Jewish Community 1787-1883*. 1994.
21 These parishes are identified by M in the list in Chapter 5.
22 Mr J Roberts, 52 St Andrews Road, Sutton Coldfield, West Midlands, B75 6UH.
23 Godber. *Op cit.* pp 50-51.
24 Daniel & Samuel Lysons. *Magna Britannia. Vol I, Pt I. Bedfordshire*. 1813.
25 Samuel Lewis. *A Topographical Dictionary of England*. 1831.
26 Colin R Chapman. *The Growth of British Education & Its Records*. Lochin Publishing. 1992.
27 Colin R Chapman. *Ecclesiastical Courts, Officials & Records: Sin, Sex & Probate*. Lochin. 1997.
28 British Record Society. Vols 10-11, 18, 25, 43-44, 54, 61, 67-68, 71-72, 74-77, 80-81, 83, 100.
29 Frederic A Blaydes. *Genealogia Bedfordiensis*. 1890.
30 Principal Registry of the Family Division, Somerset House, The Strand, London WC2R 1LP until mid-1998 and thereafter at First Avenue House, High Holborn, London WC1V.
31 Northamptonshire Record Office, Wootton Hall Park, Northampton, NN4 8BQ.
32 Birmingham District Probate Registry, Cavendish House, Waterloo Street, Birmingham, B2 5PS.
33 CRO/BFHS. *Bedfordshire Parish Poor Law Papers 1622-1834*. Occasional Paper 2. 1991.
34 Christopher J Pickford. *BFHS Journal*. Vol 9 No 3, pp 20-22. Autumn 1993.
35 Historical Manuscripts Commission, Quality Court, Chancery Lane, London WC2A 1HP.
36 In classes ASSI 31 to 39, HO 23, HO 140, HO 27, HO 17, HO 18, HO 19 respectively.
37 Colin R Chapman. *Tracing Your British Ancestors*. Lochin Publishing. 1996.
38 John M Burgoyne, Lt-Col Sir. *Regimental Records of the Bedfordshire Militia (1759-1884)*. 1884.
39 Colin R Chapman. *Tracing Your British Ancestors*. Lochin Publishing. 1996.

Postscript - Recording Your Research

Having discovered numerous details on your ancestors, or families or communities in which you are interested, you should organise these into a form that others can share and enjoy the fruits of your research. Writing a family or local history need not be arduous but the results will be most satisfying. Handwritten or computer generated genealogies and family histories enable your work to be appreciated by a wider audience. You may even consider publishing your efforts. Guidance on recording and writing up a family history is given in the Chapman Records Cameo *Tracing Your British Ancestors* [39].

Index